MW01474290

GEORGIAN COLLEGE LIBRARY

GEOB-BK
$52.65

STORES AND RETAIL SPACES 12

From the Retail Design Institute
and the Editors of *VMSD* magazine

**Library Commons
Georgian College
One Georgian Drive
Barrie, ON
L4M 3X9**

ST MEDIA GROUP INTERNATIONAL
Cincinnati, Ohio

© Copyright 2011, ST Media Group International Inc.

All rights reserved. No part of this book may be reproduced in any form without written permission of the copyright owner. All images in this book have been reproduced with the knowledge and prior consent of the individuals concerned. No responsibility is accepted by the publisher for any infringement of copyright or otherwise, arising from the contents of this publication. Every effort has been made to ensure that credits accurately comply with information supplied.

ISBN 10: 0-944094-70-8
ISBN 13: 978-0-944094-70-9

Published by:
ST Books, a division of ST Media Group International Inc.
11262 Cornell Park Drive | Cincinnati, Ohio 45242
P: 513-421-2050 | F: 513-744-6999 | E: books@stmediagroup.com
www.bookstore.stmediagroup.com

Distributed outside the U.S. to the book and art trade by:
Collins Design, an Imprint of HarperCollins Publishers
10 East 53rd Street | New York, NY 10022
www.harperdesigninternational.com

Design by Kim Pegram, Sr. Art Director, *VMSD, Hospitality Style, Boutique Design*
Written by Anne DiNardo Editor, *VMSD* (except as noted)
Edited by Matthew Hall, Editor, *Boutique Design*
Source lists and index by Taylor Douglas Hall

Printed in China
10 9 8 7 6 5 4 3 2 1

STORES AND RETAIL SPACES 12

For 40 years, retailers, designers and architects from all over the world have entered their finest projects in the *VMSD* International Store Design Competition. Members of the Retail Design Institute gather to determine the best in retail design excellence from a variety of diverse submissions.

Here are those recognized winners from two *VMSD*/Retail Design Institute International Store Design Competitions, judged in November 2009 and 2010, and published in *VMSD* in February 2010 and 2011, respectively.

TABLE OF CONTENTS

2010 RDI COMPETITION WINNERS

- 8 Brown Thomas Luxury Hall
- 12 Niketown New York World Basketball Festival Retail
- 14 Lotte Gwangbok Department Store
- 16 La Boutique Palacio
- 20 Liverpool Polanco
- 22 Bloomingdale's Santa Monica
- 24 Bloomingdale's Dubai
- 28 Man Studio
- 30 Wenger – Maker of the Genuine Swiss Army Knife
- 32 Merrell Concept Prototype
- 34 Hot Topic
- 38 Carlo Pazolini
- 42 SAQ Signature
- 44 Levi's Flagship Store
- 46 Tiffany & Co.
- 48 The Flagship Store Powered by Reebok
- 52 ALLSAINTS Spitalfields
- 54 SABBABA – food music & friends
- 56 GUU Izakaya
- 58 Spring Rolls - Conestoga
- 60 Doltone House, Darling Island Wharf
- 62 The Culinary Institute of America Campus Store/ Tasting Teaching Facility
- 64 The Landmark
- 66 Longo's Brothers Fruit Markets
- 70 Legacy Landing Fueling and Convenience Store
- 72 Donato Spa + Salon
- 76 Centura
- 80 The Exchange
- 82 Eyewear from the Beginning to the Future Exhibition
- 84 Nike Mobile Unit for the World Basketball Festival

2009 RDI COMPETITION WINNERS

- 88 The Hudson's Bay Co. – The Room
- 92 Brown Thomas & Co. – Men's Tailoring and Contemporary Department
- 94 Liverpool
- 96 Barneys New York
- 100 Neiman Marcus
- 104 Zu + Elements
- 106 Magico Imperial
- 108 Timberland
- 110 Maska
- 112 225 Forest
- 116 Murale
- 118 Ralph Lauren
- 122 Diesel
- 124 Barbie
- 128 West Elm
- 132 Blushberry
- 134 Paris Baguette
- 136 Spring Rolls – Fairview
- 138 McEwan
- 142 Bravo Supermercado
- 146 Souk Du Soleil
- 148 Sassoon
- 150 First Financial Bank
- 152 Snaidero USA Showroom
- 156 Fornari Group Headquarters
- 158 West Marine Jacksonville
- 162 Christian Dior Temporary Store

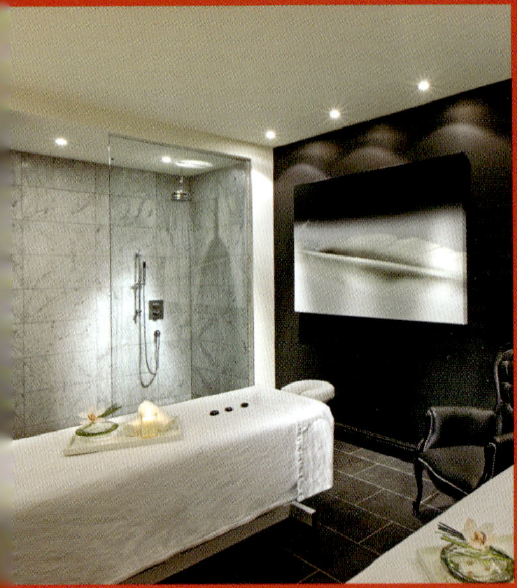

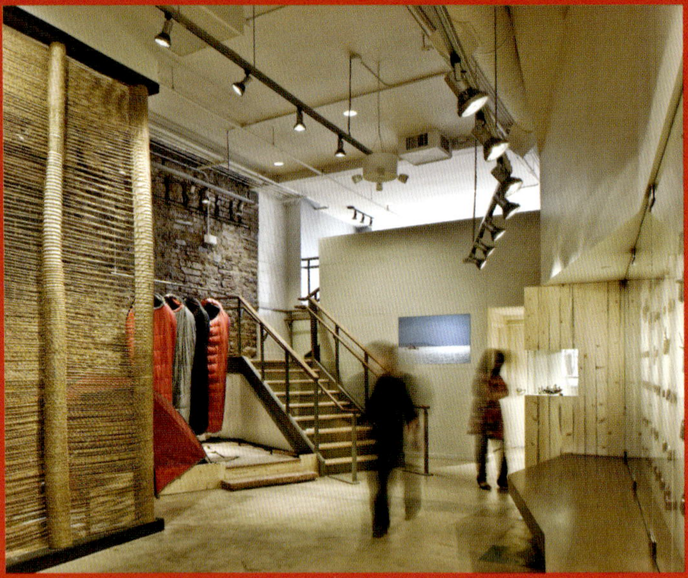

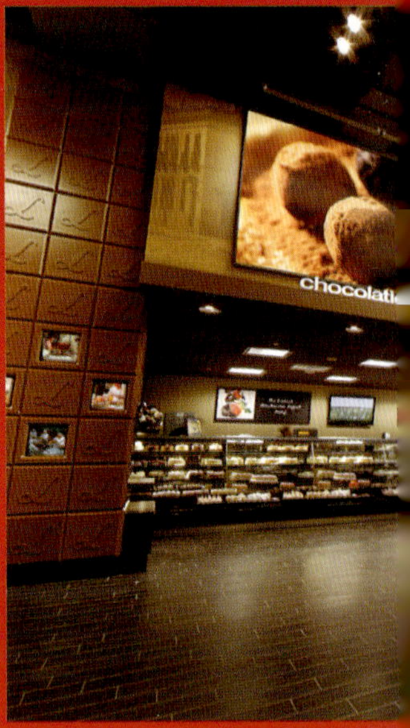

2010 WINNERS

BROWN THOMAS LUXURY HALL
DUBLIN

First Place / Innovative Materiality

Brown Thomas Luxury Hall didn't need the luck of the Irish to win top honors in RDI's annual store design competition. Just a dazzling array of materials, lighting and natural colors to create a world of refined luxury.

Its Dublin Street Flagship has been an established landmark in Ireland since the 1840s, earning its place on the international stage of luxury retailing. When the retailer wanted to evolve its offering to include a new department featuring fine watches, jewelry and luxury gifts, designers sought to create a space that would transport shoppers to a luxurious setting while still staying grounded to its Irish heritage.

"We needed to create a space that was iconic on a global point of view," says Diego Burdi, creative partner, Burdifilek (Toronto), the firm that designed the award-winning space.

Inspired by the country's natural richness, designers introduced a soft color palette, feminine design aesthetics and what Burdi calls "feats of engineering" to create an 8500-square-foot department that's a delight to the senses.

Among the riches are honed Italian marble flooring in mottled creamy shades, columns clad in tinted antiqued mirror and seamless, semi-circular glass display cases in soft polished nickel that appear to float over champagne-colored Starfire glasses bases.

Perimeter walls in dichroic glass reveal a shimmering, gold-hued iridescence.

"When you look at it all together, it speaks beautifully and demographically to where the store is situated," says Burdi.

– Anne DiNardo

RETAILER Brown Thomas Luxury Hall, Dublin
DESIGN Burdifilek, Toronto; Diego Burdi, Creative Partner; Paul Filek, Managing Partner; Tom Yip, Project Manager; Jeremy Mendonca, Senior Designer; Jacky Ngan, Project Manager Intermediate; William Lau, Designer Intermediate; Helen Chen, Designer; Anthony Tey, Senior CAD Production; Edwin Reyes, CAD Production; Amy Chen, CAD Production; Wilson Lau, CAD Production
PHOTOGRAPHY Ben Rahn, Toronto

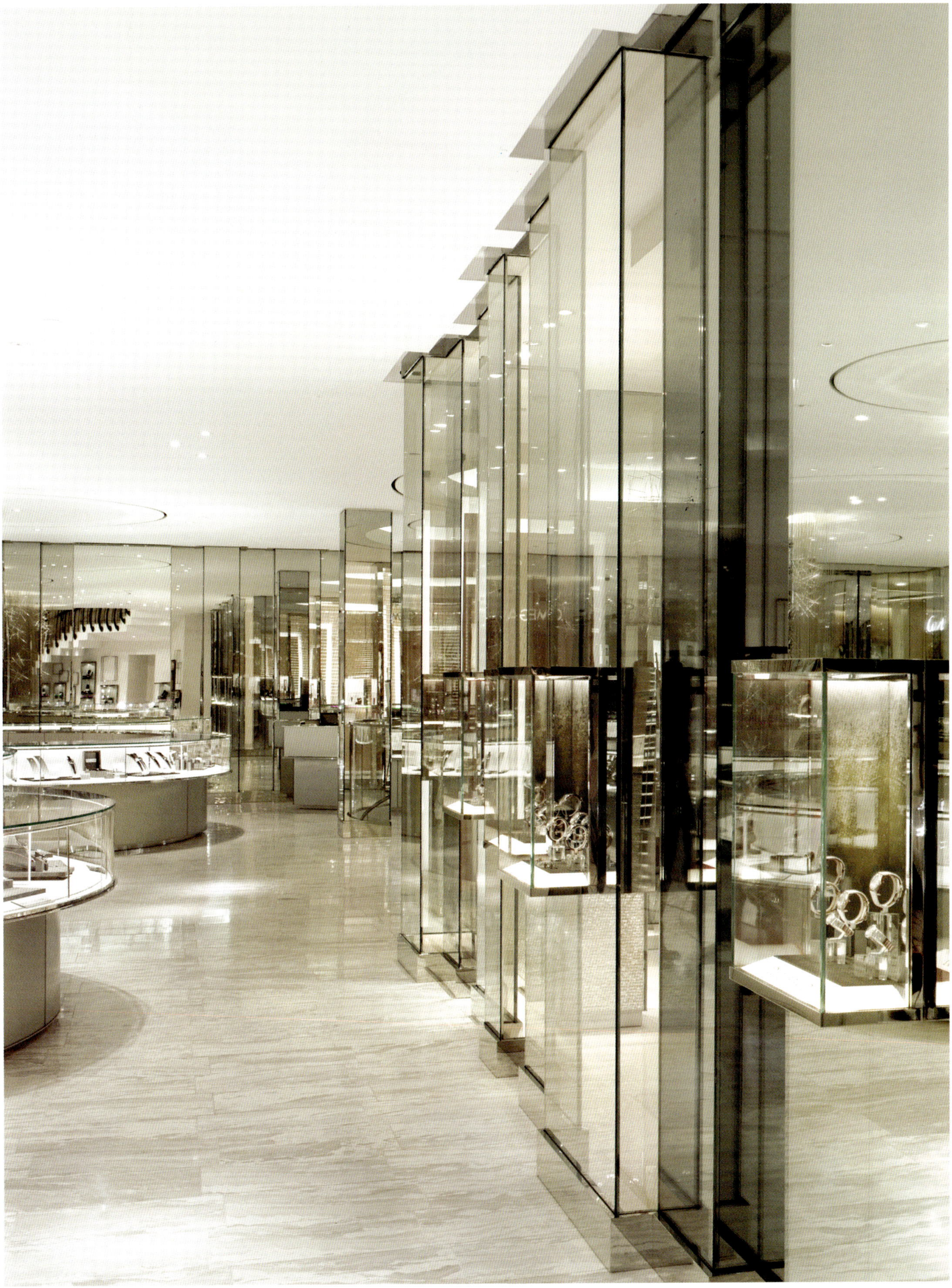

BROWN THOMAS LUXURY HALL
DUBLIN

NEW FLOOR OR SHOP WITHIN AN EXISTING DEPARTMENT OR SPECIALTY STORE

STORES AND RETAIL SPACES 12

NIKETOWN NEW YORK WORLD BASKETBALL FESTIVAL RETAIL
NEW YORK

Award of Merit / Innovative Signage/Graphics

Niketown brought the game of basketball to life inside its New York flagship when it created the largest retail expression for its first World Basketball Festival. Fixtures and graphics were designed and manufactured for this first floor space, where Nike, Brand Jordan and Converse were displayed side-by-side together for the first time.

The store's street window was opened up in back to allow a view into the 7200-square-foot area, which housed a tee destination and footwear area.

Seventeen-foot tall foam sculptures of basketball stars suspended in mid-dunk action hung inside the atrium, creating a sense of courtside action.

RETAILER Niketown New York World Basketball Festival Retail
DESIGN LIT Workshop Inc., Portland, Ore.
PHOTOGRAPHY Nike Inc., Beaverton, Ore.

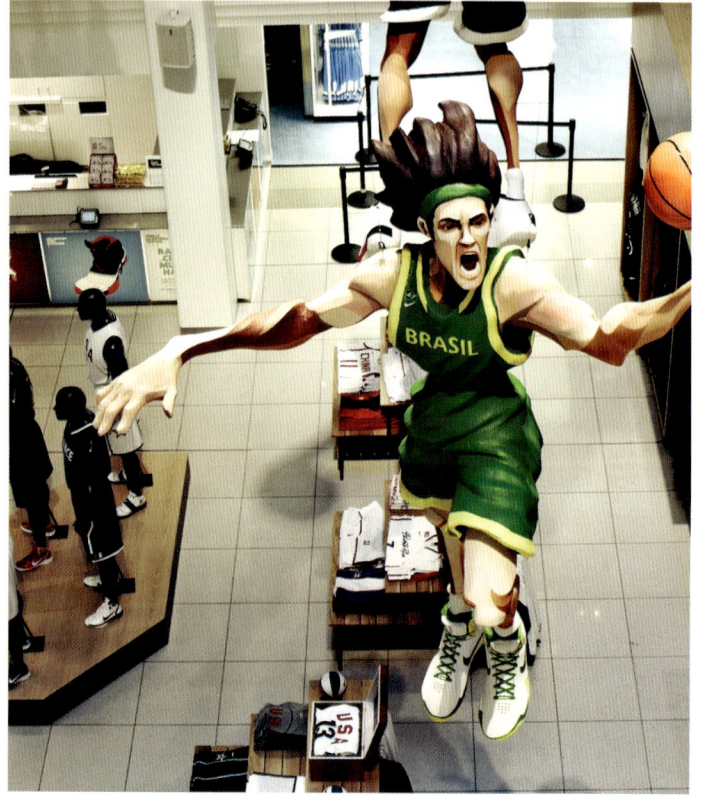

STORES AND RETAIL SPACES 12

LOTTE GWANGBOK DEPARTMENT STORE

BUSAN, SOUTH KOREA

First Place

Department-store giant Lotte is transforming Busan's Gwangbok Harbor District with its waterfront development that includes a new signature, 11-floor department store.

Inspired by its seaside location, the design's centerpiece is a sculpture of 10,000 fishlike shapes suspended from the ceiling and descending over the atrium through all the surrounding floors.

To reinforce a theme of fluidity, the design includes broad, wavelike arcs in the floor and ceiling patterns; partitions with kelp-like descending bands; decorative lighting in irregular lines of blue neon; and globular chairs that might suggest rocks on the sea floor.

– *Tom Zeit*

RETAILER Lotte Department Stores – Seoul
DESIGN ID& Design International, Fort Lauderdale, Fla.; Sherif Ayad, President/Creative Director; Jae Kyung Kim, Project Manager/Senior Designer; Olfat Ayad, Senior Designer; Brent Cartwrigh, Senior Designer; Mervet Ayad, FF&E/Designer; Wendy Wright Griffin, Designer; Roberto Mercado, Rendering; Jamie Guillen, Technical Director; Carlos Granada, Technical Coordinator; Jairo Castaneda, Design Production; Brian Saponaro, Design Production; Diana Santiago, Production; Claudia Frias, Production; Lauren Adams, Lighting Coordinator/Production; Heather Feitz, Lighting
PHOTOGRAPHY ID& Design International, Fort Lauderdale, Fla.

STORES AND RETAIL SPACES 12

LA BOUTIQUE PALACIO
MEXICO

Award of Merit

Mexico's prestigious department store, El Palacio de Hierro, wanted to create a smaller, more edited specialty store brand, La Boutique Palacio, for fashion and home collections.

An open fashion floor uses organic forms to allow shoppers to flow from one curved shop to another. The home floor features a semi-open area with a large central great room for furniture vignettes surrounded by individual spaces for home fashions. Each focal point includes a mix of fashion, signature furniture and accent lighting to create memorable lifestyle settings.

RETAILER La Boutique Palacio, Mexico
DESIGN PDT International LLC, Fort Lauderdale, Fla.; Fernando Castillo, Creative Director
FLOORING Island Stone, Pompano Beach, Fla.; Milliken Constantine Carpet, Miami; Porcelanosa, Miami; Shaw Contract Group, Miami
STONE Marble of the World, Fort Lauderdale, Fla.
TEXTILES Maharam, Miami; Maya Romanoff, Dania, Fla.
WOOD Tabu, Vero Beach, Fla.
PHOTOGRAPHY Dana Hoff, West Palm Beach, Fla.

STORES AND RETAIL SPACES 12 17

LA BOUTIQUE PALACIO

MEXICO

STORES AND RETAIL SPACES 12   19

LIVERPOOL POLANCO
MEXICO CITY

Award of Merit

Liverpool's Mexico City flagship was built in the 1970s and had been partially updated over the years. To reflect the department store's new brand positioning as a world-class contemporary flagship store, designers employed a mix of timeless white architecture, black accents and Liverpool's pink brand color. Large porcelain and wood tiles accent the floor. New focal areas and fixturing allow for cross merchandising and elevated visual displays.

RETAILER Liverpool Polanco, Mexico City
DESIGN FRCH Design Worldwide, Cincinnati; James R. Lazzari, Chief Architectural Officer; Barb Beeghly, Vice President, Planning & Merchandising; Steve Gardner, Vice President; Young Rok Park, Design Director; Claudia Cerchiara, Project Director; HeeSun Kim, Design Director; Rob Carey, Senior Designer; Deb Casey, Planning & Merchandising, Documentation; Ric Gerke, CAD Production; Carol Osterbrock, Senior Resource Designer
LIGHTING Lighting Workshop Inc., Brooklyn, N.Y.
PHOTOGRAPHY Christian Dohn, Cincinnati

STORES AND RETAIL SPACES 12 | 21

BLOOMINGDALE'S SANTA MONICA
SANTA MONICA, CALIF.

First Place

Eclectic fixturing, retractable Chinese lantern-style dressing room pods, local artwork and a mix of materials create the specialty-store setting of Bloomingdale's Santa Monica Place. Inspired by the brand's SoHo store, an abundance of natural light and weathered wood contrasted with glass and glazed concrete reference the new beachside setting. Even Bloomingdale's iconic black-and-white checkerboard floor was reinterpreted as stenciled concrete inside the two-level store. Exposed ceiling areas allow for trellis-like canopies to delineate spaces, which include cosmetics, accessories and men's on the main floor and women's sportswear on the second.

RETAILER Bloomingdale's Santa Monica, Santa Monica, Calif.
DESIGN Mancini-Duffy, New York; Ed Calabrese, Creative Director; Lisa Contreras, Resource Director; Marian Crawford, Project Manager; Stan Kao, Senior Designer; Courtney Kemper, Project Designer; George Winsper, Job Captain, 1st Floor; Alex Mai, Job Captain, 2nd Floor
FIXTURING Faubion Associates, Dallas, Tex.; Stanly Fixtures Company, Inc., Norwood, N.C.; Bullder's Furniture Ltd., Winnipeg, Canada; Bruewer Woodwork Mfg. Co., Cleves, Ohio
FLOORING Atlas Carpet, New York; Architectural Systems Inc., New York
FURNITURE AND UPHOLSTERY Barrett Hill, New York; Vaswani, Union, N.J.
LIGHTING Lighting Workshop, New York
WALLCOVERINGS Carnegie Fabrics, Rockville Centre, N.Y.; Wilsonart, Temple, Tex.
PHOTOGRAPHY Gray Crawford, Sante Fe, N. Mex.

STORES AND RETAIL SPACES 12　23

BLOOMINGDALE'S DUBAI

DUBAI, U.A.E.

Award of Merit

Bloomingdale's has had its greatest successes in fashionable U.S. cities like New York and San Francisco. But perhaps no U.S. city has the appreciation for Western fashion elegance, or the ability to pay for it, that Dubai has. It's fitting, then, that Bloomingdale's very first international store opened at the Dubai Mall.

To accommodate certain space challenges, the Bloomingdale's Dubai store is actually two separate spaces: a 146,000-square-foot fashion store and a 54,000-square-foot home store. The locations "look very Bloomingdale's" with black and white floors, black lacquer and mirror finishes, luxurious fitting rooms, illuminated mannequin platforms, long sightlines, lots of original artwork and the use of furniture in place of fixtures in some places. Arabic influences are tenderly cushioned throughout the store as highlights.

– Steve Kaufman

RETAILER Bloomingdale's, Dubai, U.A.E.
DESIGN Callison/RYA, Seattle, Wash.; John Von Mohr, Creative Director; Denny Will, Production Manager; Kimberly Mayrhofer, Project Designer; Alecia Avent, Project Designer; Jack Hruska, Executive Vice President for Creative Services with Bloomingdale's
CARPET Constantine, Calhoun, Ga.
FLOORING Architectural Systems Inc., New York
FURNATURE Minotti, Meda, Italy; Ligne Roset, Milan, Italy; Donghia, Mount Vernon, N.Y.; Barbara Barry By Henredon, Morganton, N.C.; De Sede, Klingnau, Switzerland
LIGHTING Moooi, Breda, Netherlands; Donghia, Mount Vernon, N.Y.; Jean De Merry, West Hollywood, Calif.; Cavalli, Bologna, Italy; Ingo Maurer, Munich, Germany; Brand Van Egmond, A.H. Naarden, Netherlands; Flos, Bovezzo, Italy; Kenzo, Singapore; Amerlux, Fairfield, N.J.
WALLCOVERINGS Maya Romanoff, Skokie, Ill.; Anya Larkin, Long Island City, N.Y.; Carnegie Fabrics, Rockville Centre, N.Y.; Maharam, New York
PHOTOGRAPHY Chris Eden, Seattle

STORES AND RETAIL SPACES 12 25

BLOOMINGDALE'S DUBAI
DUBAI, U.A.E.

STORES AND RETAIL SPACES 12   27

MAN STUDIO
SEOUL

First Place

Today's modern man wants a store where he can tune-up his look. Enter Man Studio, in Seoul's Hondgae area, dedicated entirely to beauty and wellness for the XY chromosome.

To create a masculine environment where shoppers would feel comfortable, the store features tool-box fixtures with internal illuminated display tops, exposed brick walls, rusty steel panels and concrete and black lacquer finishes. Dramatic spotlighting adds a moody, raw edge. Props, including motorbikes, maps, compasses and cameras, appeal to the well-traveled man.

RETAILER Man Studio, Seoul
DESIGN JHP, London; David Rook; Patrick Volavka
PHOTOGRAPHY Jinju Kang, Seoul

STORES AND RETAIL SPACES 12

WENGER – MAKER OF THE GENUINE SWISS ARMY KNIFE
BOULDER, COLO.

First Place / Innovative Space Planning

In 2009, the 116-year-old Wenger Brand decided to branch out with its first U.S. retail flagship. The retailer selected a site at the Pearl Street Mall, which was built in the early 1900s, and chose to reuse as much of the envelope as possible, including the existing wood floor, ceiling and stone walls, to illustrate the brand's history of authenticity, value, multi-functionality and love of outdoor adventure. LED light fixtures were chosen for their energy efficiency. Beetle-kill pine reinforces a local sustainability message while stainless steel celebrates the material that serves as the basis of every Swiss Army knife.

RETAILER Wenger – Maker of the Genuine Swiss Army Knife, Boulder, Colo.
DESIGN Gensler, Denver, Colo.; Blake Mourer, Design Director; Glenna Tyndall, Project Manager; Jenny West, Interior Designer; JD Praeger, Project Architect; Harry Spetnagel, Graphic Designer
PHOTOGRAPHY Gensler, Denver, Colo.

STORES AND RETAIL SPACES 12 | 31

MERRELL CONCEPT PROTOTYPE
ROCKFORD, MICH.

Award of Merit

Look, listen and touch – that's the message inside Merrell's latest store design, which invites customers to explore their senses. All the merchandise is accessible to shoppers. A perimeter sliding-door fixture keeps open stock on the floor and is covered in outdoor graphic photography. A topography wall fixture can be changed to feature the latest products and a curated wall near the entrance invites customers to share testimonials or items that might have been collected while using a Merrell product.

RETAILER Merrell Concept Prototype, Rockford, Mich.
DESIGN FRCH Design Worldwide, Cincinnati; Christian Davies, Vice President & Creative Director; Monica Gerhardt, Account Manager; Scott Rink, Project Manager; Cathleen Bunker, Senior Interior Designer; Lori Koithoff, Resource Design Director; Aaron Ruef, Senior Graphic Designer
PHOTOGRAPHY Wolverine World Wide Inc., Rockford, Mich.

STORES AND RETAIL SPACES 12   33

HOT TOPIC
SANTA MONICA, CALIF.

Award of Merit

Hot Topic turns up the volume with in-store technology that brings social and technological components into the shopping experience. Unique twisted acrylic prisms in the storefront windows reflect projected images that mirror the display on the back wall screen. A staging area transitions between performance and retail space, with a ceiling metal grid, LED-embedded stage floor, theatrical lights and a green room that functions as a portable fitting room or clearance area. A new t-shirt wall has a stadium-like configuration that curves up to the ceiling and houses monitors showing live concert clips. Shoppers can also access online music using Hot Topic's ShockHound and co-create micro-manufactured tunes as well as their own t-shirt designs.

RETAILER Hot Topic
DESIGN JGA, Southfield, Mich.; Ken Nisch, Chairman; Mike Curtis, Creative Director
CEILINGS Greneker, Los Angeles
FIXTURES Laurel Manufacturing, Delanco, N.J.; Kosakura, Santa Ana, Calif.
FLOORING Floricpolytech, Parker, Ariz.; Dwyer Marble & Stone, Farmington Hills, Mich.
GLASS D & R Glass, Rancho Cucamonga, Calif.
LIGHTING CRI, Fairfield, N.J.; David Gilman; Charlie Morrison
PAINT AND LACQUER General Coatings Corp., Rancho Cucamonga, Calif.
SIGNAGE Blake Signs, Stanton, Calif.
UPHOLSTERY Dazian, Burbank, Calif.
PHOTOGRAPHY Bielenberg Associates, Los Angeles

STORES AND RETAIL SPACES 12 35

HOT TOPIC
SANTA MONICA, CALIF.

SPECIALTY STORE 1501 TO 3000 SQUARE FEET

STORES AND RETAIL SPACES 12   37

CARLO PAZOLINI
MILAN

First Place (tie) / Innovative Conceptual Design

Carlo Pazolini's flagship at Piazza Cordusio in Milan redefines the luxury shoe and accessories shopping environment with cellular shoe displays that seem to peel away from the walls. Swarm intelligence algorithms are used to arrange the wall displays, forming loose cellular structures. The shelving and seating cells are made using a glueless molding process, which bonds natural wool felt with the polymer at a molecular level, creating a new structural composite. High ceilings and large window openings bring this play of color, material and shape out onto the busy plaza.

RETAILER Carlo Pazolini, Milan
DESIGN Giorgio Borruso Design, Marina Del Rey, Calif.; Giorgio Borruso, Principal Designer
LIGHTING RemaTarlazzi S.p.A., Sforzacosta Macerata, Italy
PHOTOGRAPHY Alberto Ferrero, Milan

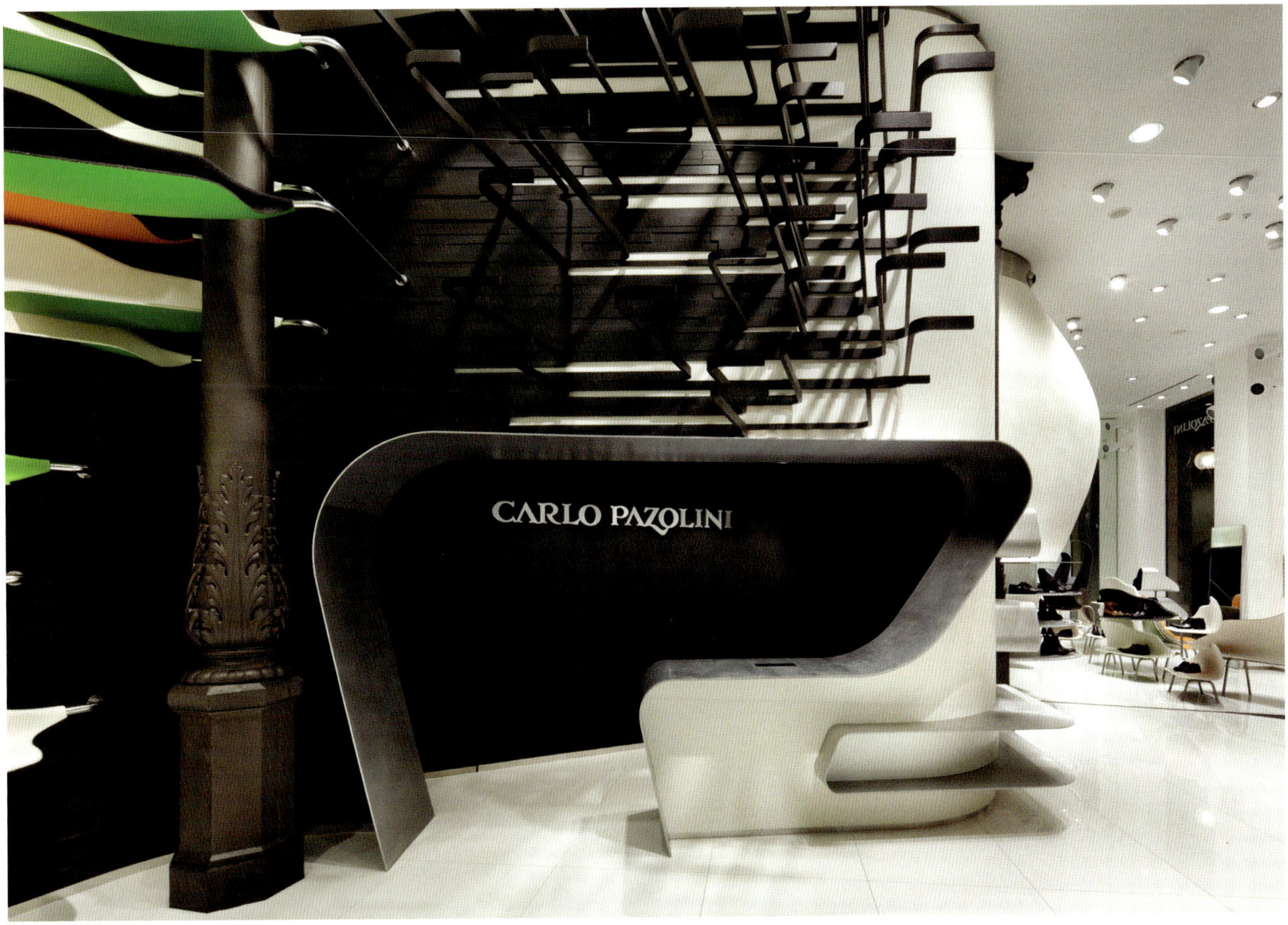

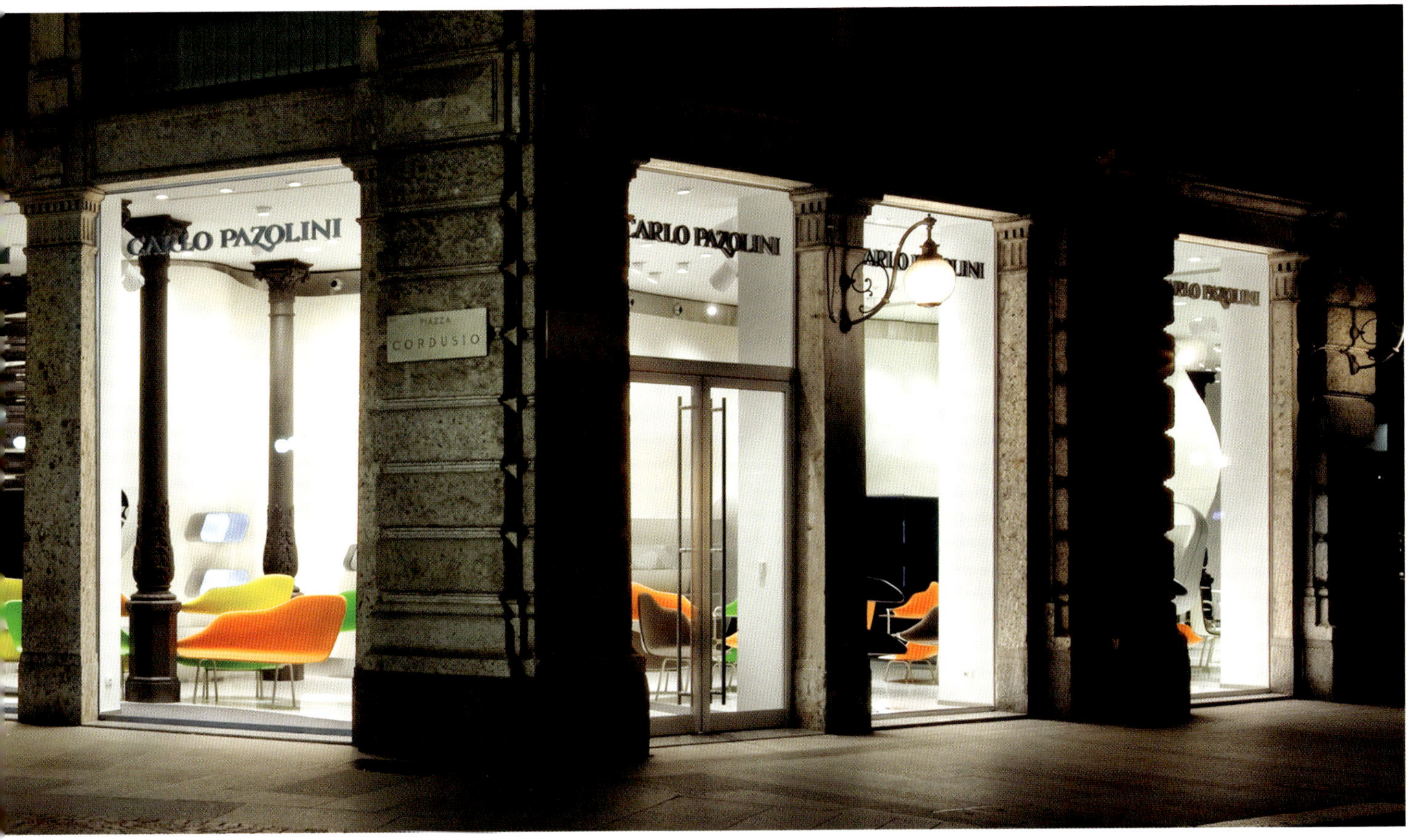

CARLO PAZOLINI
MILAN

STORES AND RETAIL SPACES 12   41

SAQ SIGNATURE
QUEBEC CITY, QUE.

First Place (tie)

Quebec Liquor Board's Signature banner serves connoisseurs and aficionados. The new concept for this 5000-square-foot space is inspired by an authentic château wine cellar of yesterday built with modern-day materials and techniques. A large spiral glass, steel and slate staircase transports shoppers from the ground floor Selection store to the upper-end space above, accented with coat of arms and quotations from famous poets. Materials, including earthy polished concrete floors, massive pillars clad in black slate and two custom suspended glass cellar showcases, add to the setting. Champagne gets its own setting, with birch wall units and limestone walls that echo the color of bubbly and further tie in with the French château theme.

RETAILER SAQ Signature, Quebec City, Que.
DESIGN Aedifica Inc., Montreal; SidLee, Montreal; Societe des Alcools du Quebec Planning and Design, Montreal
FLOORING AND WALLS TechnoProfil, St-Nicolas, Que.
GRAPHICS SidLee, Montreal; Imafix, Terrebonne, Que.
LIGHTING Litemor, Montreal
PHOTOGRAPHY SidLee, Montreal

STORES AND RETAIL SPACES 12   **43**

LEVI'S FLAGSHIP STORE

LONDON

First Place

Levi's sought to create the ultimate jeanswear destination by taking London shoppers and visitors on a journey through the origins of denim and the evolution of its brand. The ground floor Origins gallery hosts art exhibits and live music performances, alongside seasonal and promotional ranges. Designers created a factory-inspired setting with reclaimed regency brick, concrete, wood, wired glass, raw steel, indigo oak doors and cream-enameled metals. The Inspection Room houses a sea of denim where customers can shop by fit or finish, with specific lines displayed on tailor's forms that sit above contemporary haberdasher's cabinets.

RETAILER Levi's Flagship Store, London
DESIGN Checkland Kindleysides, Leicester, UK; Jeff Kindleysides, Founder; Joe Evans, Associate Design Director; Maggie Wright, CAD Design Manager; Hana Carter, Senior Project Manager; Karen Robertson, Senior Project Manager; Richard Dunkin, Projects Director; John Churton, Head of Procurement
LIGHTING Erco Lighting Ltd., London
PHOTOGRAPHY Keith Parry, London

STORES AND RETAIL SPACES 12 45

TIFFANY & CO.
SHANGHAI, CHINA

Award of Merit

The legendary jeweler sought to reinvent its flagship experience with an innovative and glamorous design on Shanghai's Huai Hai Road. The iconic blue gift box inspired a façade composed of soft translucent layers of shimmering pale blue glass on the upper floors and clear and opaque bronze glass and glittering metal patterned screens on the lower portion. Inside, various types of glass were highlighted using traditional artisan techniques, such as eglomise, silver leaf and glass etching. A marble, walnut and bronze staircase rises through the space encircling a suspended crystal glass chandelier.

RETAILER Tiffany & Co., Shanghai, China
DESIGN S. Russell Groves Architects, New York; Russell Groves; Neal Beckstedt; Stacey Bertin; Brett Tipert; Lyn Weiss; Rachel Saletel; Harper Halprin; Pamela Ledesma; Corey Schneider; Luke Hellkamp; Sylwia Olewicz; Sherman Adams; Bader Kassim
PHOTOGRAPHY S. Russell Groves Architects, New York; Chen Zhang Ging, Shanghai

STORES AND RETAIL SPACES 12   47

THE FLAGSHIP STORE POWERED BY REEBOK

EAST RUTHERFORD, N.J.

Award of Merit

This 9600-square-foot retail space serves fans of both the New York Giants and Jets at the new Meadowlands Stadium. The store can transform from one team to the other in about three hours, using a combination of team-specific LED lighting fixtures set against a primarily white backdrop and flooring. Digital sign-age, including a large LED video wall, can be programmed to play a specific team's footage. And revolving peri-meter display panels pivot to show either Jets or Giants merchandise, while a cap tower near the back of the store uses hinged cover panels to flip merchandise.

RETAILER The Flagship Store Powered by Reebok, East Rutherford, N.J.
DESIGN Chute Gerdeman, Columbus, Ohio; Denny Gerdeman, Founder and CEO; Brian Shafley, President and Chief Creative Director; Wendy Johnson, EVP, Account Management; Corey Dehus, Creative Director, Brand Communications; Steve Pottschmidt, Director, Design Development; Rob Turner, Senior Designer, Retail Environments; Steve Johnson, Senior Designer, Graphic Production; Katie Clements, Designer and Materials Specialist
FLOORING Retroplate Systems, Provo, Utah; Sherwin Williams, Cleveland, Ohio; Johnsonite, Chagrin Falls, Ohio
FIXTURES OPTO International Inc., Wheeling, Ill.
LIGHTING X-nth, Maitland, Fla.
PAINT AND LACQUER ICI Paint; Sherwin Williams, Cleveland, Ohio
PLASTIC LAMINATE Formica Laminate, Cincinnati
WALLCOVERINGS Crane Composites; Wolf-Gordon Inc.; Rosul and Associates, Lakewood, Ohio
PHOTOGRAPHY Mark Steele Photography, Columbus, Ohio

STORES AND RETAIL SPACES 12   **49**

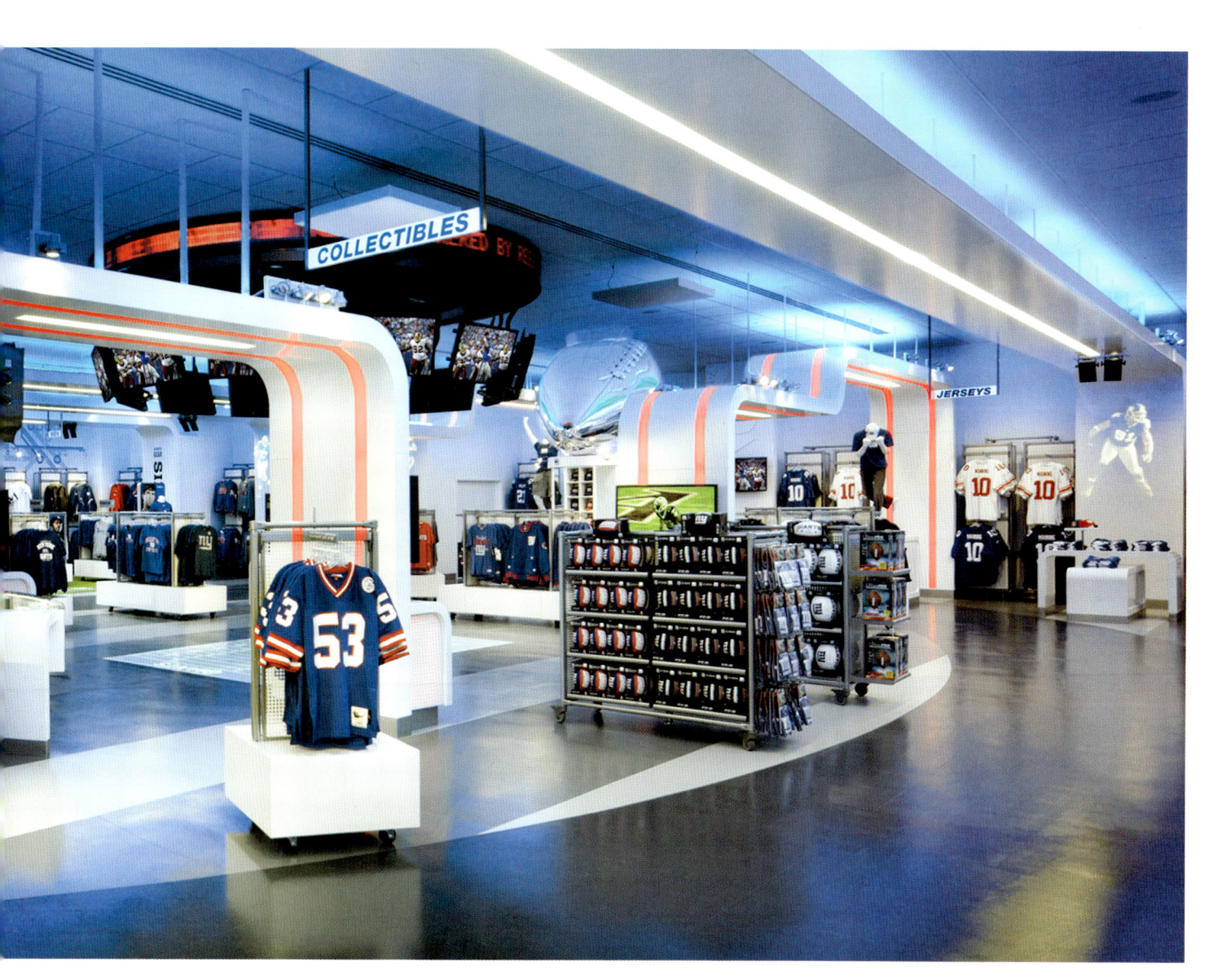

THE FLAGSHIP STORE POWERED BY REEBOK

EAST RUTHERFORD, N.J.

STORES AND RETAIL SPACES 12 | 51

ALLSAINTS SPITALFIELDS
NEW YORK

First Place / Innovative Fixture Design / Innovative Visual Merchandising

AllSaints' home in New York's SoHo neighborhood is a great study in reuse and repurposing. Antique printing presses, looms and Singer sewing machines provide an abundance of visual delights throughout the three-story space. All freestanding fixtures are made of reclaimed items that are modified to fit, including tables, sewing machines, garment factory equipment and gears. Pipe and rail, steel-threaded rods and wood and glass-inset display shelves form perimeter fixtures that stay true to the brand identity while offering a heightened visual presence.

RETAILER AllSaints Spitalfields, Soho Store
DESIGN 212 Design Inc., New York; Insite Development; RTS Contracts Ltd.
FLOORING Reclaimed French white oak
LIGHTING PRG-Vision Quest Lighting, New Windsor, N.Y.
PHOTOGRAPHY Hal Horowitz, New York

52 SPECIALTY STORE OVER 10,001 SQUARE FEET

STORES AND RETAIL SPACES 12   53

SABBABA – FOOD MUSIC & FRIENDS
NEWTOWN, AUSTRALIA

First Place

Redefining the fast-food experience, designers chose to create an interior with an open-kitchen environment that doesn't divide the food from the customers. Tables are set nearby for views to the food-prep area. Utilizing a neutral color palette that would highlight the vibrant colors from the dishes, the walls are clad in solid timber straps and paneling. Floor tiles are a mix of colored concrete with a Mediterranean blue highlight in a check-pattern to add depth and definition to the space. Custom fixtures are detailed with metal and hand-painted timbers to further accentuate the character of the space.

RETAILER Sabbaba – Food Music & Friends, Newtown, Australia
DESIGN Otto Design Interiors, Summer Hill, Sydney
PHOTOGRAPHY Caroline Fualkowski, Sydney

54 SPECIALTY FOOD COURT OR COUNTER-SERVICE RESTAURANT

STORES AND RETAIL SPACES 12   55

GUU IZAKAYA
TORONTO

First Place

Making its Toronto debut, Guu is an authentic Japanese "izakaya," or pub, which started in Vancouver. The small, informal eatery features communal tables, benches and bar seating for a variety of experiences. A continuous wall-to-ceiling structure of reclaimed wood wraps one end of the venue for a more private setting. Traditional Japanese design elements can be found in the grid-like arrangement of the platinum slate tiles. However, a juxtaposition of raw and new materials adds a modern twist to this Zen environment, such as an assortment of exposed bulbs hanging at various heights. On the exterior, a smooth platinum gray slate storefront contrasts with a heavy weathered wooden door.

RETAILER Guu Izakaya, Toronto
DESIGN dialogue 38 Inc., Toronto; Bennett Lo, Principal; Raul Delgado; Wendy Wang
FLOORING Stonetile, Toronto
LIGHTING Matthew Birch, Toronto; Contrast Lighting Group, Montreal
STONE AND TILE Primestone, Toronto; Rivalda, Toronto
WALLCOVERINGS Ronald Redding Wallcovering; Metro Wallcovering, Mississauga, Ont.
WOOD Matthew Birch, Toronto
PHOTOGRAPHY Eric Lau, Toronto

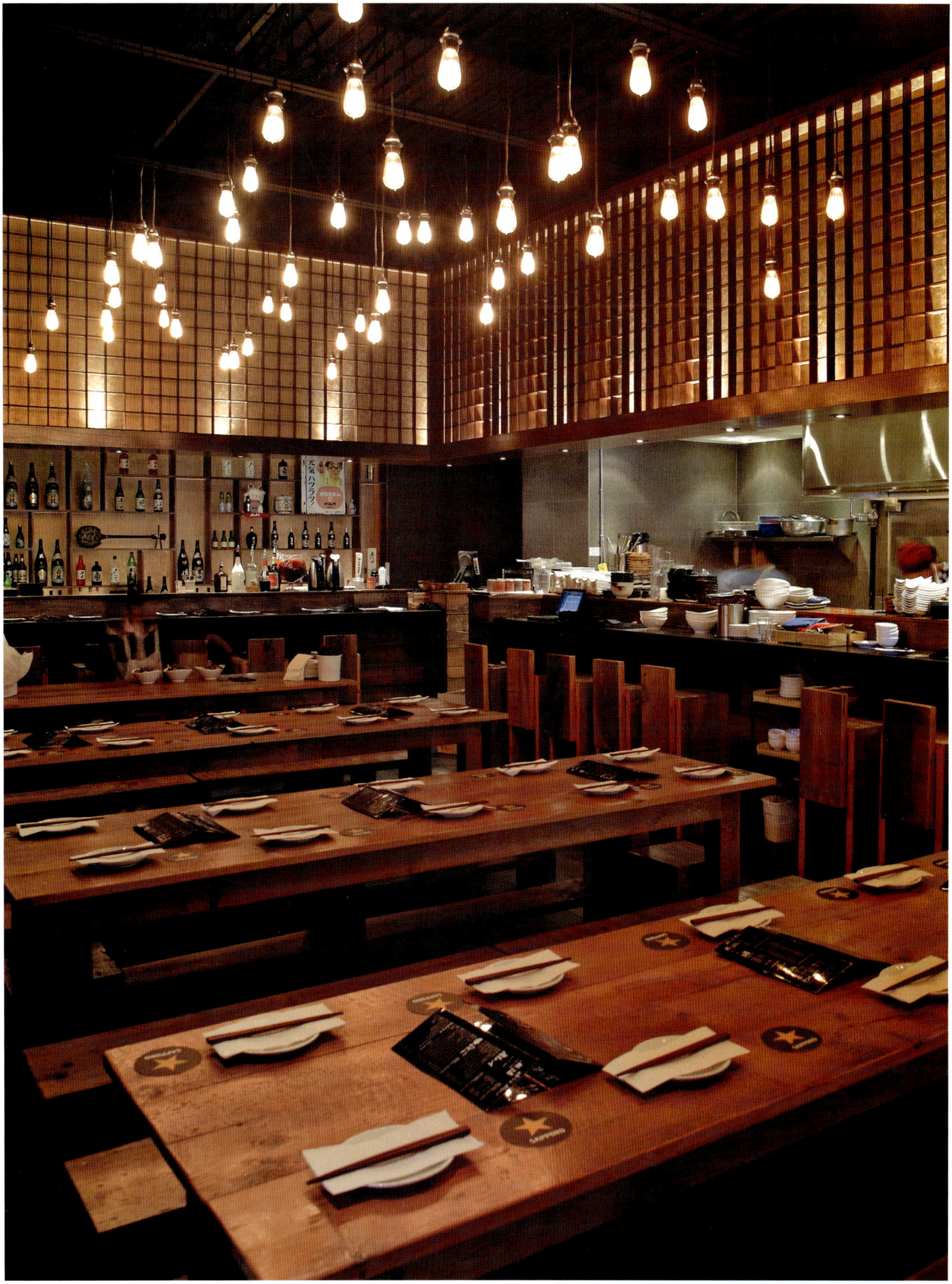

SPRING ROLLS
WATERLOO, ONT.

Award of Merit / Innovative Lighting Design

As this Pan-Asian chain continues to expand westward throughout Canada, it's employing a variety of lighting treatments to create a vibrant dining experience. Color-changing LEDS draw attention through the red aluminum slats of varying widths applied to the restaurant exterior. Inside the bar and lounge area, a custom lighting fixture above the bar is crafted of Mylar film that reflects the activity within the space. In the dining room, a 24-by-3-foot chandelier is composed of multiple rows of 8-foot-long strands of internally illuminated crystals.

RETAILER Spring Rolls, - Conestoga, Waterloo, Ont.
DESIGN dialogue 38 Inc., Toronto; Bennett Lo, Principal; Raul Delgado; Marya Hwyn; Wendy Wang
FLOORING Stonetile, Toronto
STONE AND TILE Ciot., Toronto
WALLCOVERINGS Vecom America; Metro Wallcovering, Mississauga, Ont.; Maharam, Toronto
PHOTOGRAPHY Eric Lau, Toronto

STORES AND RETAIL SPACES 12 **59**

DOLTONE HOUSE, DARLING ISLAND WHARF

SYDNEY

First Place

The design of this waterfront fresh-food emporium was based on the theater. An Italian kitchen takes center stage with satellite activities, including a deli, onsite cooking school and café, contributing to a holistic experience. Imported polished marble, polished concrete, bronze aluminum, steel and stone materials provide a contemporary take on traditional Italian themes. Flexible fixturing designs present bulk produce straight off the palet, while refrigeration and display counters are integrated into custom joinery with high-end details.

RETAILER Doltone House, Darling Island Wharf, Sydney
DESIGN Geyer Pty Ltd., Sydney; Melinda Huuk, Project Leader; Allan Griffiths, Project Coordinator; Hayden Crawford, Designer; Tim Giles, Designer; Louise Mackrill, Designer
PHOTOGRAPHY Jason Loucas, Sydney

STORES AND RETAIL SPACES 12 **61**

THE CULINARY INSTITUTE OF AMERICA CAMPUS STORE/TASTING TEACHING FACILITY

ST. HELENA, CALIF.

Award of Merit

Designers recovered the original warehouse interior of a former winery to create a state-of-the-art complex that involves a new campus store, olive oil and chocolate tasting facilities, teaching kitchens and café. Discrete cabinetry displays merchandise while still allowing exposed views of the historic building fabric. In areas that needed to be enclosed, bamboo in a horizontal pattern was applied to distinguish them from the building's original finishes. All utilities, including electrical, mechanical and plumbing, were congregated into a central "pot rack" trunk duct, which also serves as a directional guide through the space. Materials reflect the culinary arts, including stainless steel, maple butcher block and glass.

RETAILER The Culinary Institute of America Campus Store/ Tasting Teaching Facility, St. Helena, Calif.
DESIGN Miroglio Architecture and Design; Oakland, Calif.; Joel Miroglio, Design; Patrick Ahearn, Associate; Nailesh Jhaveri, Associate
PHOTOGRAPHY David Wakely Photography, San Francisco

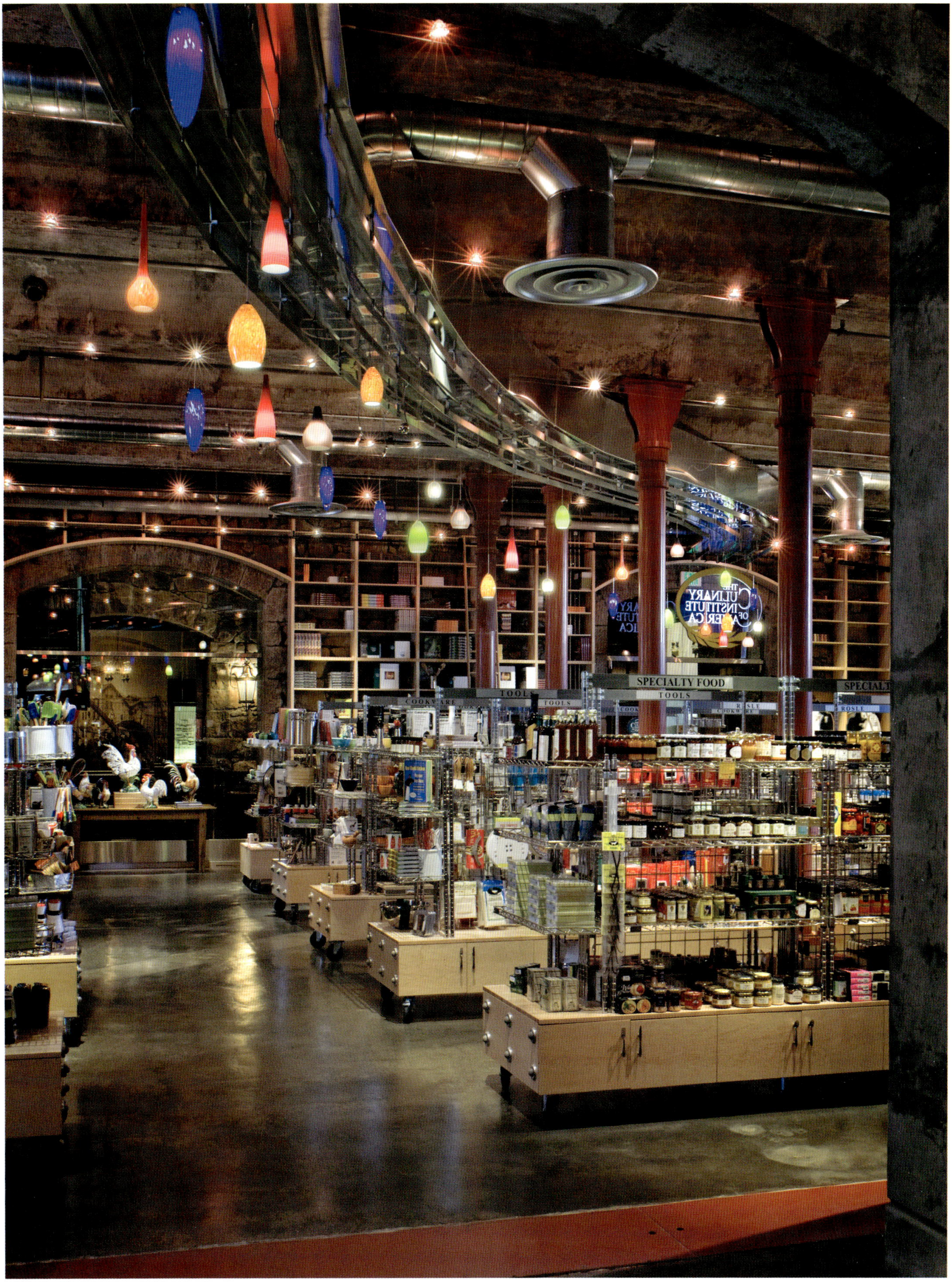
SPECIALTY FOOD
TOOLS

THE LANDMARK
MANILA, PHILIPPINES

First Place

The renovation of the 76,500-square-foot supermarket inside Landmark's Manila department store had to overcome several challenges, including an average ceiling height throughout the space of just 11 feet. And, work in the Philippines restricts the use of wood because of heavy deforestation in the area.

So designers employed a strategic use of graphics and materials to create a modern, airy and easy-to-navigate space. Elements include a wall of colored glass tiles in the wine department and decorative vertical accents, such as graphics applied on glass or strips of colored glass, in the meat and produce areas. To create a sense of spaciousness, the ceilings were painted black and accented with a series of hanging light-colored floating planes.

RETAILER The Landmark - Makati, Manilla, Phillippines
DESIGN Hugh A. Boyd Architects, Montclair, N.J.; Hugh A. Boyd, FAIA; A. Henderson Boyd; JoAnn Montero
FLOORING Architectural Materials Supplies Trading Ltd., Hong Kong
LIGHTING The Lighting Practice, Philadelphia, Pa.; Ping Hao Lighting, Zhongshan, China
PHOTOGRAPHY Toto Labrador, Quezon City, Philippines

STORES AND RETAIL SPACES 12   65

LONGO'S BROTHERS FRUIT MARKETS INC.
TORONTO

Award of Merit

For Longo's first full-format supermarket in Toronto, designers were confronted with an irregular store footprint, multiple entry points and a basement location. To draw shoppers in, a dynamic light feature greets shoppers at the entry. The lighting element can also change colors according to what's in season. Graphic-wrapped columns and shadow boxes serve as integrated communication vehicles, while bulkheads throughout the store feature digitally printed wallpaper of food images and inspirational words. Dark walnut fixtures in the produce area and Caesar stone countertops add a fresh, natural look to the space.

RETAILER Longo's Brothers Fruit Markets, Toronto
DESIGN Watt International, Toronto; Glen Kerr, Team Lead, Interior Designer; Paulis Ciskevicius, Interior Designer; Sam Chan, Interior Designer; Matt DeAbreu, Illustration; Bryan Morris, Graphics; Ash Pabani, Graphics; Eliza Tang, Graphics; Shahla Mulji, Account Manager
CERAMIC TILE Olympia Tile, Toronto
PAINT AND LACQUER Benjamin Moore, Toronto
PHOTOGRAPHY Si Hoang, Toronto

STORES AND RETAIL SPACES 12

LONGO'S BROTHERS FRUIT MARKETS INC.
TORONTO

STORES AND RETAIL SPACES 12   69

LEGACY LANDING FUELING AND CONVENIENCE STORE

AIRWAY HEIGHTS, WASH.

Award of Merit

The layout of this 5000-square-foot convenience store was developed around the idea of drive-up service at opposite ends, with main retail amenities in the center. Fluorescent pendant fixtures provide general lighting while suspended tracklights highlight wall signage. Mini-pendants add a decorative touch over transaction areas. Signage identifies major product categories, such as "Fountain," "Dairy," and "Frozen." Built-in shelving was used at transaction counters to spotlight vendor-supplied products, while custom black gondola units and grab-and-go refrigerated and non-refrigerated units create an uncluttered environment.

RETAILER Legacy Landing Fueling and Convenience Store, Airway Heights, Wash.
DESIGN Wolfe Architectural Group, Spokane, Wash.; Licia LeGrant, Architect
CARPET Shaw Contract Group, Cortersville, Ga.
FABRICS Architex, Northbrook, Ill.
FLOORING Ibex Flooring, Spokane, Wash.
LIGHTING Columbia/Hubbell/Presolite Lighting, Greenville, S.C.; Atlantic Lighting Inc., Fall River, Mass.; Tech Lighting, Skokie, Ill.
TILE Daltile/American Olean, Dallas, Tex.
PHOTOGRAPHY Shawn Toner, Spokane, Wash.

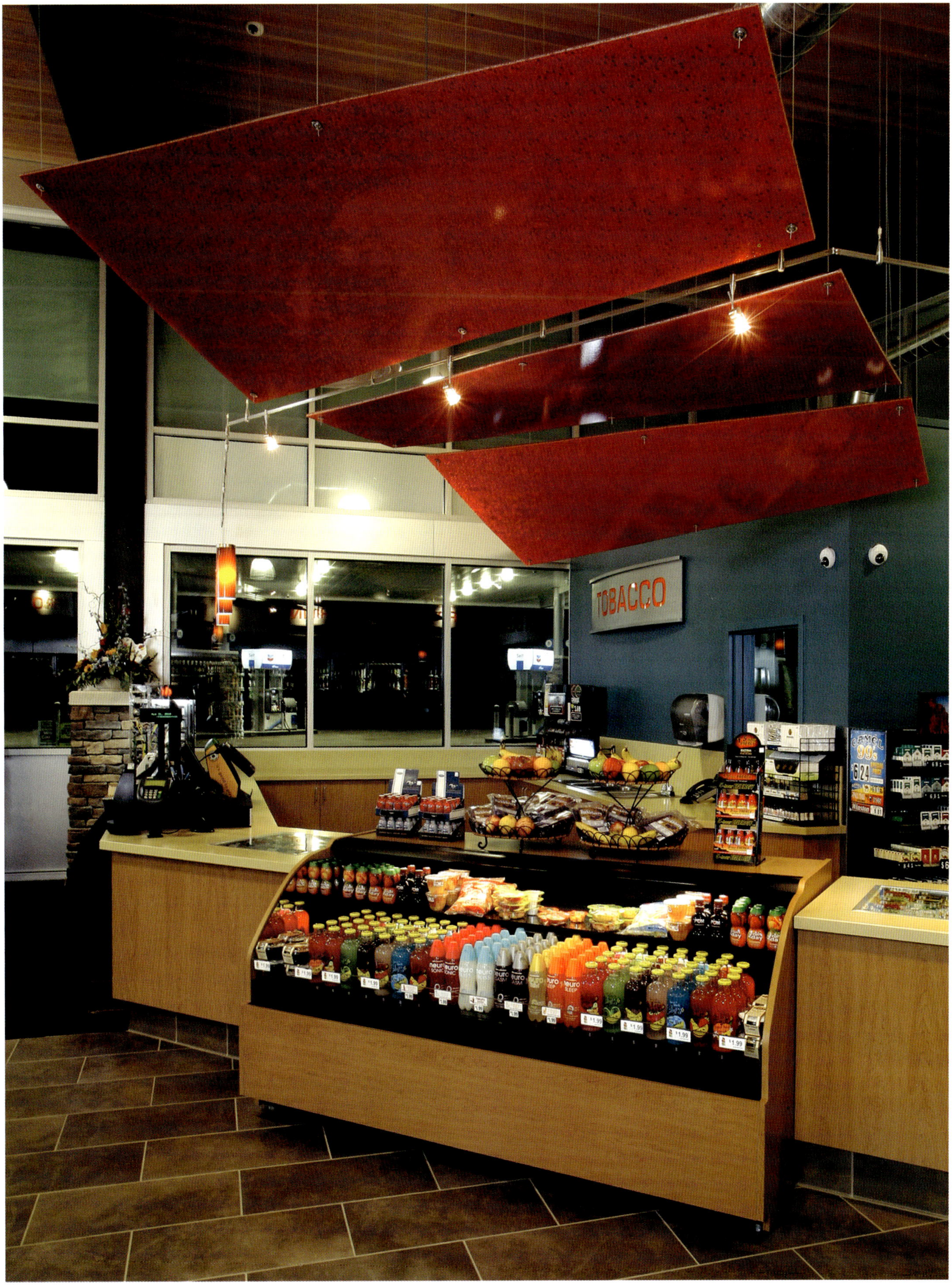
TOBACCO

DONATO SPA + SALON
TORONTO
First Place

For his new Toronto salon, owner John Donato wanted a luxurious boutique experience and flagship for his VIP and celebrity clientele that would still be inviting to anyone seeking a pampering environment. The 5400-square-foot space includes 1000 square feet of retail space, an 1800-square-foot salon and 1800 square feet for spa and back-of-house needs. French vanilla and rich ebony provide the backdrop palette highlighted by 20-arm chandeliers, stone block reception desk and woodgrained porcelain tile flooring in a herringbone pattern. Two custom-designed graphic artwork panels, measuring 10-by-6-feet, highlight the hair-wash station. Modern styling stations in the salon's signature black wainscoting serve as wall dividers.

RETAILER Donato Spa + Salon, Toronto
DESIGN II by IV Design Associates Inc., Toronto; Dan Menchions, Partner; Keith Rushbrook, Partner; Ken Lam, Intermediate Designer; Emillie Jones, Junior Designer; Laura Abanil, Junior Designer
FLOORING Olympia Tile, Toronto
LIGHTING Eurolite, Toronto
MARBLE AND STONE Ciot, Toronto
PHOTOGRAPHY David Whittaker

STORES AND RETAIL SPACES 12   73

DONATO SPA + SALON

TORONTO

STORES AND RETAIL SPACES 12   75

CENTURA
MONTREAL

First Place

This tile manufacturer sought to broaden its client base with a new showroom that would appeal to contractors, architects and designers, as well as upscale residential clients. Two creativity hubs are designed as open labs with work tables and wall puck systems. The open-house section near the main entrance features new products. To overcome the large volume of the 30-foot tall ceilings, designers added an oversized light sculpture in the reception lounge. The company's products are used on the flooring, while white quartzite provides the countertop surface. Green elements include a 30-foot tall living wall of English ivy and a running fountain.

RETAILER Centura, Montreal
DESIGN GHA Design Studios, Montreal; Steve Sutton, Partner; Serge Prud'homme, Project Director; France Delorme, Director of Resources
LIGHTING Futura, Ste-Therese, Que.
PHOTOGRAPHY Yves Lefebvre, Montreal

STORES AND RETAIL SPACES 12   77

CENTURA
MONTREAL

STORES AND RETAIL SPACES 12 **79**

THE EXCHANGE
TINKER AIR FORCE BASE, OKLAHOMA CITY, OKLA.

First Place

To provide military personnel and their families with a fresh, updated shopping experience, design firm Chute Gerdeman Retail organized The Exchange into three areas: home, life and style. A V-aisle layout is designed to attract customers to branded lifestyle destinations of PowerZone electronics and BeFit activewear. The materials palette includes high-polish concrete floors, dark woods, gleaming whites and high-gloss graphics on modified shipping containers. The entire store is modular, with every fixture and architectural element mobile, per military project mandate. The 20-foot tall focal walls on hidden wheels define the softline departments with 12-foot tall color frames. Five specialty boutique shops are made of stylized versions of super-scale shipping containers.

RETAILER The Exchange, Oklahoma City, Okla.
DESIGN Chute Gerdeman, Columbus, Ohio; George Nauman, Principal and Chief Marketing Officer; Brian Shafley, President and Chief Creative Director; Wendy Johnson, EVP, Account Management; Adam Limbach, Vice President, Brand Communications; Mindi Trank, Director, Brand Strategy; David Birnbaum, Architect, Design Development; Elaine Evans, Senior Designer, Brand Communications; Renee Kinkopf, Designer, Brand Communications; Steve Johnson, Senior Designer, Design Implementation; Rob Turner, Senior Designer, Retail Environments; Katie Clements, Designer and Materials Specialist
FABRICS CF Stinson, Rochester Hills, Mich.
FLOORING Scofield, New Castle, Ind.; Amtico International, Atlanta, Ga.; J&J-Invision, Dalton, Ga.; Construction Specialties, Muncy, Pa.; Atmosphere Recycled Flooring; Daltile
LIGHTING All Modern Lighting, Boston, Mass.; Western Extralite, Kansas City, Mo.; Get Back Inc., Oakville, Conn.; T-Trak by Tech Lighting; Alluminare
PAINT AND COATINGS Tiger Drylac, St. Charles, Ill.; Sherwin Williams; Benjamin Moore
WALLCOVERINGS DL Couch, New Castle, Ind.
WOOD PRODUCTS DPI- Decorative Panels Inc., Toledo, Ohio; Advantage Trim and Lumber Co.; Common Lumber
PHOTOGRAPHY Mark Steele Photography, Columbus, Ohio

STORES AND RETAIL SPACES 12 | 81

EYEWEAR FROM THE BEGINNING TO THE FUTURE EXHIBITION

VANDERBILT HALL, GRAND CENTRAL TERMINAL, NEW YORK

First Place / Innovative Conceptual Design

This temporary installation for a museum exhibition was designed to display historic through contemporary and prototype eyewear. Giorgio Borruso Design sought to rethink the glass display case as a fractal, inhabitable "city" with a large abstracted convex glass lens that was cut by a series of vectors that connect various architectural and programmatic elements. Ten-inch thick bands of clear acrylic were geometrically cut to reveal the items. Graphic acrylic surfaces are created by adding film layers and fluorescent backlit surfaces add uniform illumination. Rich colors and subtle graphics further add impact to the display.

RETAILER "Eyewear from the Beginning to the Future" Exhibition, New York
DESIGN Giorgio Borruso Design, Marina Del Rey, Calif.; Giorgio Borruso, Principal Designer
PHOTOGRAPHY Magda Biernat, New York

STORES AND RETAIL SPACES 12 | 83

NIKE MOBILE UNIT FOR THE WORLD BASKETBALL FESTIVAL
MORE THAN 20 LOCATIONS THROUGHOUT NEW YORK

Award of Merit

To promote the World Basketball Festival, transit buses were converted into mobile stores by cutting off the roof, extending the sides outward, adding skylights and creating an 8-by-10-foot entrance. Reclaimed pieces of basketball court accented the walls and floor, while exterior bus graphics featured images of players. To add a museum-like quality to the space, the uniforms of several of the countries participating in the festival were on display. Interactive elements included a colorful shoe display, including shoe samples and color options, which invited visitors to design their own footwear.

RETAILER Nike Mobile Unit for the World Basketball Festival, New York
DESIGN Czarnowski, Chicago
PHOTOGRAPHY Nike Inc., Beaverton, Ore.

STORES AND RETAIL SPACES 12　85

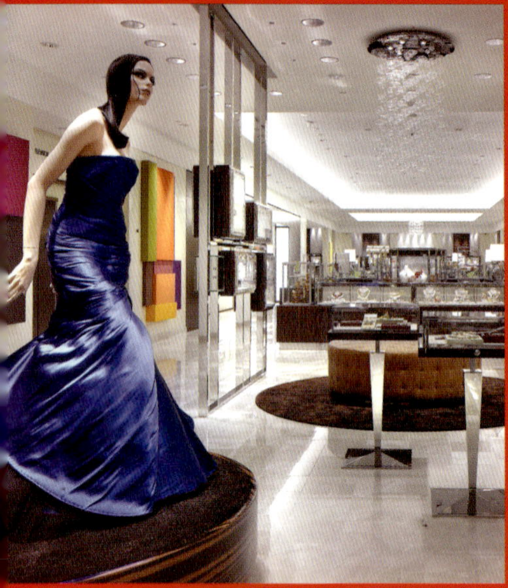
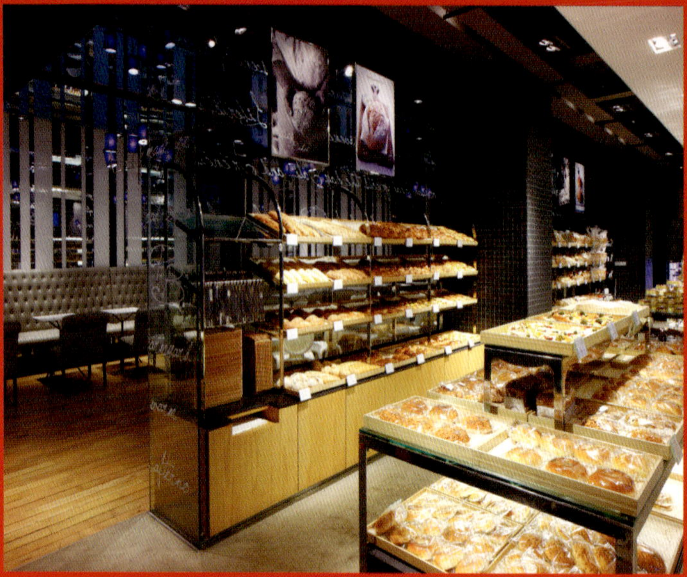
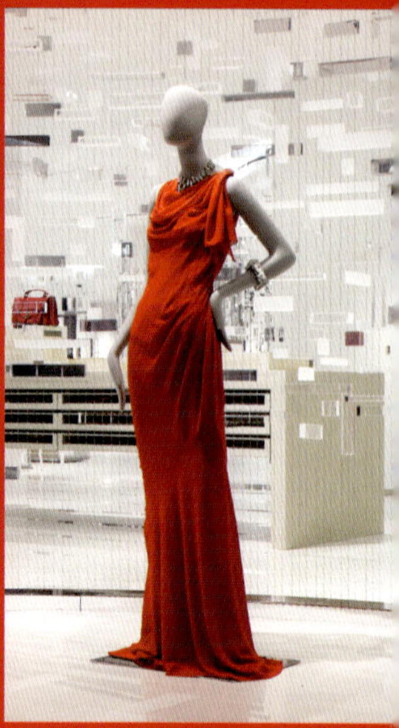

2009 WINNERS

THE HUDSON'S BAY CO.'S — THE ROOM

TORONTO

First Place

During its heyday in the '70s and '80s, the St. Regis Room (now called The Room) at Hudson's Bay Co. was *the* place for international apparel. Design firm Yabu Pushelberg gave The Room a refresh with a simple palette of white, polished metal, high-gloss lacquer and glass. Three floor-to-ceiling screens, each featuring different geometric shapes, curve around to create smaller areas for product presentation while still allowing broad vistas throughout the 22,000-square-foot department. Fused-glass tables, industrial chandeliers and a wall of white subway tiles provide a subtle change of style toward the back of the room. In one corner, shoes literally shine on a curved wall of internally lit shelves. Above, painted-on panels with antler motifs are one of the few references to the room's past formality.

RETAILER The Hudson's Bay Co. – The Room, Toronto
DESIGN Yabu Pushelberg, Toronto
PHOTOGRAPHY Evan Dion, Toronto

STORES AND RETAIL SPACES 12   89

THE HUDSON'S BAY CO.'S — THE ROOM

TORONTO

STORES AND RETAIL SPACES 12 **91**

BROWN THOMAS & CO. – MEN'S TAILORING AND CONTEMPORARY DEPARTMENT
DUBLIN

First Place
Innovative Store Planning

To create a distinctly masculine space for Brown Thomas' male shoppers, designers referenced the distinguished heritage of bespoke tailoring and men's fashion in Europe using a rich materials palette of Makassar ebony, charcoal brown, oyster white and marble flooring. Custom fixturing includes oceanic blue display tables. A solid walnut wall sculpture was hand carved to mimic the draping of fabric. The textures and rich tones of the tailoring area are contrasted with the contemporary zone's more playful and fashion-forward wares, allowing each area to stand out.

RETAILER Brown Thomas & Co. – Men's Tailoring and Contemporary Department, Dublin
DESIGN Burdifilek, Toronto; Diego Burdi, Creative Partner; Paul Filek, Managing Partner; Jeremy Mendonca, Senior Designer; Helen Chen, Designer; William Lau, Designer; Anthony Tey, Head of Production; Jacky Ngan, CAD Production; Edwin Reyes, CAD Production; Anna Jurkiewicz, CAD Production; Amy Chen, CAD Production; Tom Yip, Project Manager
CARPET Sullivan Source, Toronto
FABRICS Primavera, Toronto; Telio & Cie, Toronto
LIGHTING One Point Two, Dublin
PHOTOGRAPHY A Frame Inc., Toronto

STORES AND RETAIL SPACES 12   93

LIVERPOOL
ZAPOPAN, MEXICO

Award of Merit

Located outside Guadalajara, this 322,000-square-foot department store incorporates a neutral color palette of white, black and wood finishes with bold color accents to create an updated look. Merchandising bars suspended from the ceiling serve as a visual focal in the furniture department. In the apparel areas, the fitting rooms are designed as interactive lounges and open to the selling space. The colors within the escalator well's feather sculpture are used to represent the components of the Liverpool brand, including fashion, architecture and brand personality.

RETAILER Liverpool, Zapopan, Mexico
DESIGN FRCH Design Worldwide, Cincinnati; James Lazzari, Senior VP, Chief Architectural Officer; Claudia Cerchiara, Project Director; Young Rok Park, Design Director; Parke Wellman, Project Director, Planning & Merchandising; HeeSun Kim, Design Director; Monica Dreyer, Senior Project Manager; Y.E. Smith, VP Architect; Luanne Carleton, Architect; Ileana Saldivia, Architect; Carol Osterbrock, Senior Resource Designer; Niki DuBois, Resource Designer; Robert Carey, Senior Designer; Greg Smith, Graphic Designer; Marcellus Neel, Designer; Matt Cox, Designer & Merchandising; Julie Hess, Designer; Rick Gerke, CAD Production; Jonathan Capelle, CAD Production
PHOTOGRAPHY Javier Jarrin, OMS Photography, Cincinnati

NEW OR COMPLETELY RENOVATED FULL-LINE DEPARTMENT STORE

STORES AND RETAIL SPACES 12 **95**

BARNEYS NEW YORK
CHICAGO

First Place

Barneys New York moved across Oak Street to replace its 17-year-old Chicago flagship. The move gave the luxury specialty retailer the opportunity to pay homage to the Chicago School of architecture and the Carson Pirie Scott building on State Street with a rounded corner and five-story-high glass curtainwall. The six-story, 90,000-square-foot space also has many of the expected Barneys features — such as lots of natural light and open spaces, decorative murals and a dramatic staircase filled with mannequin tableaus. New design touches include an art deco-inspired geometric floor pattern and an ornate metal-and-mesh roof element. Barneys also entered a new chapter in its history by seeking LEED certification for the first time with the Chicago store.

– Steve Kaufman

RETAILER Barneys New York, Chicago
DESIGN Jeffrey Hutchison & Associates, New York; Jeffrey Hutchison, Principal; Agnieszka Chromicz, Project Management and Design; Luis Fernandez, Design; Jason Linde, Design; Kaydee Kreitlow, Design; Allie McKenzie, Design; Betse Ungemack, Interior Design
PHOTOGRAPHY Adrian Wilson, New York

STORES AND RETAIL SPACES 12   **97**

BARNEYS NEW YORK

CHICAGO

STORES AND RETAIL SPACES 12 **99**

NEIMAN MARCUS
BELLEVUE, WASH.

Award of Merit

This 126,000-square-foot store in The Bravern marks the luxury retailer's first Pacific Northwest store. Warm tones, glass screens and wood and metal finishes create a sense of contemporary style throughout. Custom decorative pendant lighting is used in several places, such as hand-blown glass balls cascading from the ceiling. An illuminated drum in cosmetics defines the "play station" makeup area, while the Men's Club houses glowing frosted glass discs. The Mariposa restaurant features an accent wall of polished plaster and curved screen walls with a random stick motif.

RETAILER Neiman Marcus, Bellevue, Wash.
DESIGN Charles Sparks + Co., Westchester, Ill.; Charles Sparks, President and CEO; Don Stone, EVP Account Manager; David Kow, Senior Creative Director; Stan Weisbrod, AIA, Interior Architect; Stephen Prosser, Account Coordinator; Rachel Mikolajczyk, Resource Studio Director
PHOTOGRAPHY Charlie Mayer Photography, Oak Park, Ill.

STORES AND RETAIL SPACES 12 **101**

NEIMAN MARCUS
BELLEVUE, WASH.

NEW OR COMPLETELY RENOVATED SPECIALTY DEPARTMENT STORE

STORES AND RETAIL SPACES 12

ZU + ELEMENTS
MILAN

First Place
Innovative Fixture Design

A geometry of cuts and segmented lines intersect and connect throughout this ultra-modern, 1100-square-foot store, located on the Via Verri in the heart of Milan's fashion district. A 12-foot-long glass counter blends seamlessly with the stainless steel, mirrors and geometric cut-outs. A special frame embedded in the white cement floor anchors the cantilevered structure. The back-painted red glass also pushes the envelope by creating the effect of depth. On top, one section of glass was intentionally left unpainted to create an internal display case for accessories, and the cash register is flush with the glass.

RETAILER Zu + Elements, Milan
DESIGN Giorgio Borruso Design, Marina Del Rey, Calif.; Giorgio Borruso, Principal Designer
PHOTOGRAPHY Alberto Ferrero, Milan

STORES AND RETAIL SPACES 12   **105**

MAGICO IMPERIAL
MONTREAL

First Place (tie)

Making its North American debut in Montreal, this avant-guard European brand used an overall design style based on geometry to establish itself as a hot new player in the local fashion arena. A crumpled wall in the women's area is composed of drywall set at angular planes. Gold serves as a predominant color and is found in the metal fixtures, bunk unit and mirrors, glass shelves and cashwrap. Cowhide-upholstered seating in the front of the fitting rooms adds an eclectic touch. All of the fixtures are custom, including three metal floor units called the "Spider racks." The units support the angular theme, while adding a sculptural touch to the space.

RETAILER Magico Imperial, Montreal
DESIGN Ruscio Studio, Montreal; Robert Ruscio, President and Principal Designer
PHOTOGRAPHY Leeza Studio, Montreal: Elizabeth Martel

STORES AND RETAIL SPACES 12 107

TIMBERLAND
LONDON

First Place (tie)

The outdoor brand brings its environmental beliefs to life through a textural use of recycled and repurposed materials inside this store at Westfield shopping center. The predominant wood and leather cut-off materials add a raw, handcrafted feel. Fixtures include tables from timber stacks and reclaimed furniture. The energy-efficient lighting plan features 4.65 watts per square foot used on the feature walls and pendant lamps. Timberland's iconic logo comes to life on the store façade with a lattice of reclaimed timber branches that wraps the store.

RETAILER Timberland, London
DESIGN Checkland Kindleysides, Leicester, U.K.; Henry Barnes, Account Director; Hana Long, Project Manager; Hannah Shepherd, Project Manager; Clive Hunt, Designer; Marc Epicheff, Designer; Maggie Wright, Design Development
PHOTOGRAPHY Keith Parry, London

STORES AND RETAIL SPACES 12   109

MASKA
MONTREAL

Award of Merit

Maska maximized the opportunity to move to a larger, more visible mall space at Rockland Centre by creating a new store environment that fuses classic architectural elements, including moldings and pilasters, with modern touches, such as laser-cut baroque silhouette mirrors, acrylic wall sconces and high-polished chrome fixtures. Keeping visual materials to a minimum, cut vinyl film in vivid fuchsia serves as an accent or as a logo treatment on tables, mirrors and wall graphics. The predominantly white space uses seven different light sources, including T8 fluorescents for indirect lighting, LEDs over the mirrors and chandeliers for a softer light. The use of tone-on-tone damask pattern wall coverings and high-polished porcelain floor tiles further accentuates the boutique setting.

RETAILER Maska, Montreal
DESIGN Ruscio Studio, Montreal; Robert Ruscio, President and Principal Designer
PHOTOGRAPHY Leeza Studio, Montreal: Elizabeth Martel

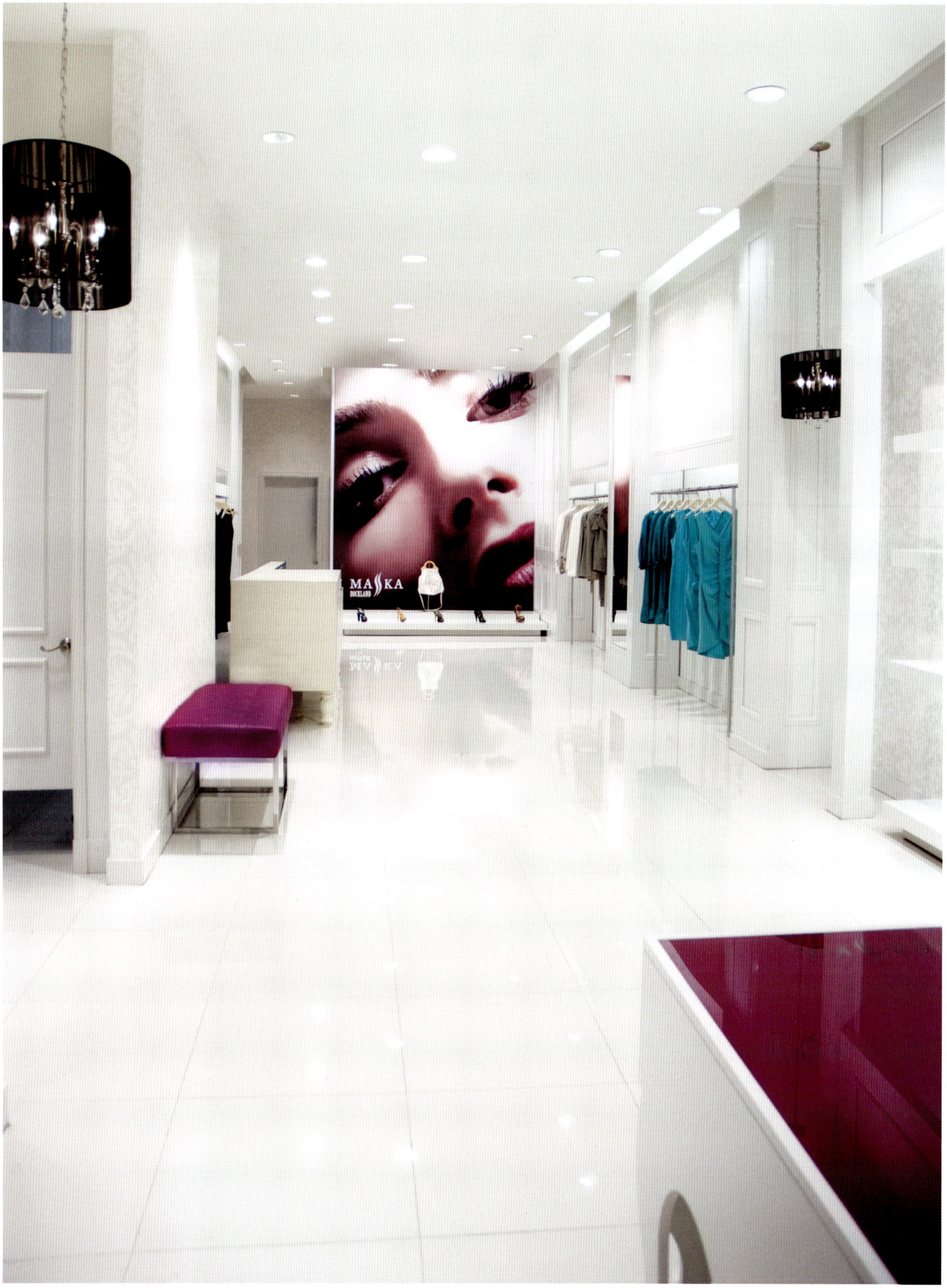
MASKA
DOCKLAND

225 FOREST
COSTA MESA, CALIF.

First Place
Innovative Visual Merchandising

Staying authentic to the lifestyle of skateboarding, surfing, music and art, this concept store was conceived as a space designed for and by kids. Located in an old warehouse, the store features a garage entry door. Plywood boards on the exterior are designed for customers to post thoughts and ideas, and once filled, the boards are moved inside the store as artwork. A contrast of raw and polished finishes are at play here, including waxed concrete flooring, plywood displays, Durock art walls and cedar-planked skylights. Salvaged fluorescent light reflectors were refitted and ganged together to create floating ceilings. To display clothing, designers chose s-hooks, workbench clamps and vintage hangers, while footwear is displayed on reused shipping pallets and apple boxes.

RETAILER 225 Forest, Costa Mesa, Calif.
DESIGN Michael Neumann Architecture LLC, New York
LIGHTING / Schwinghammer Lighting LLC, New York
PHOTOGRAPHY Sharon Risedorph, San Francisco

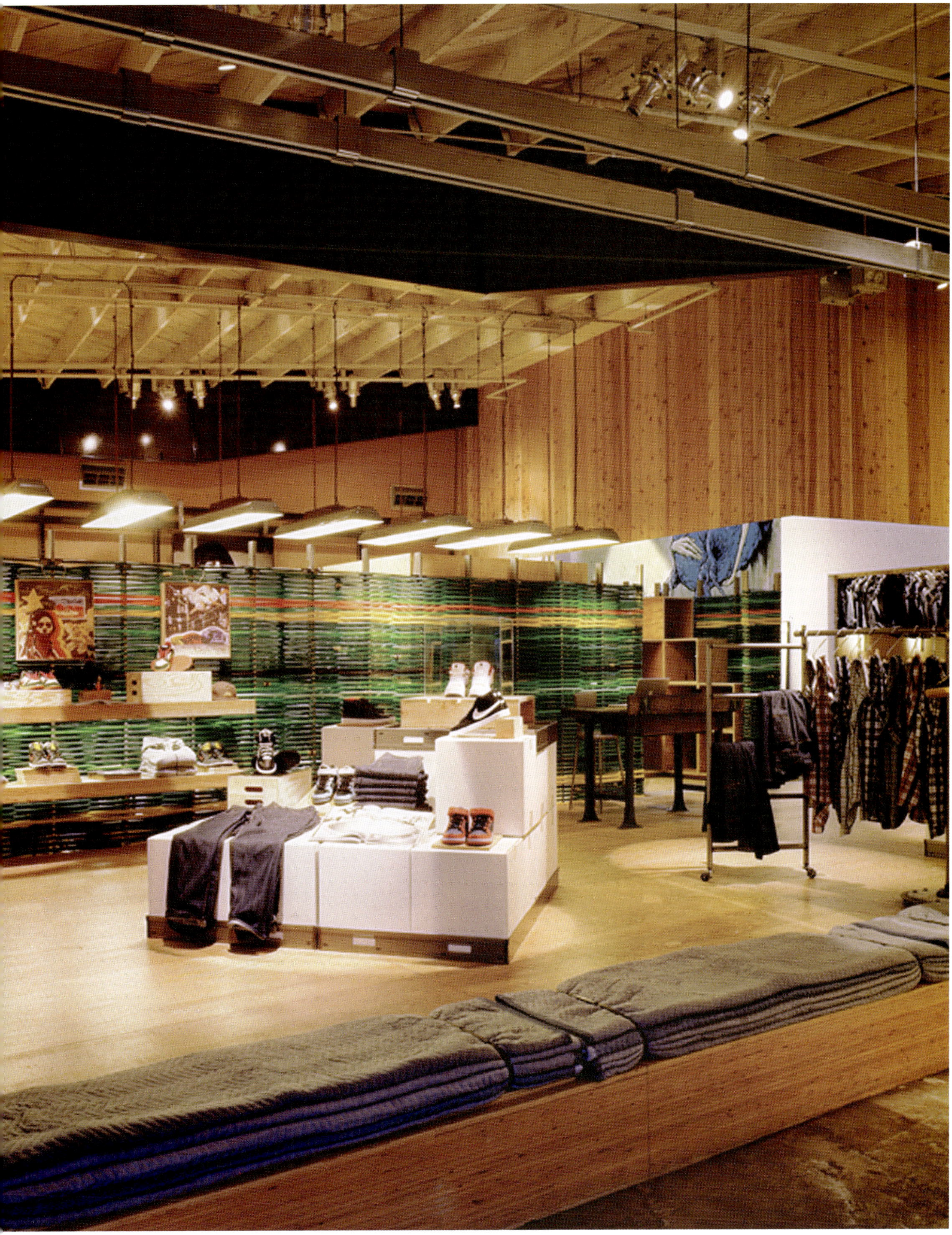

225 FOREST
COSTA MESA, CALIF.

STORES AND RETAIL SPACES 12 **115**

MURALE
MONTREAL

First Place

Open sightlines and architectural screens create a sense of pause and draw customers through this beauty retail space. Clear Starfire glass fins lit by LEDs define the derma area and act as a focal point in the rear of the store. Custom-tinted purple and blush-colored translucent elements are paired with white-on-white fixtures and matte and glossy finishes. Since lighting is such an important element in cosmetic and skincare retailing, designers incorporated ambient light washes and direct lighting to ensure precise color rendering. A kinetic light installation on the back wall includes curved translucent sand-blasted acrylic panels and LEDs to reference water and its calming properties, while adding a sense of movement to the space.

RETAILER Murale, Montreal
DESIGN Burdifilek, Toronto; Diego Burdi, Creative Partner; Paul Filek, Managing Partner; Jeremy Mendonca, Senior Designer; Helen Chen, Designer; William Lau, Designer; Mariko Nakagawa, Designer; Jacky Ngan, CAD Production; Edwin Reyes, CAD Production; Anna Jurkiewicz, CAD Production; Anthony Tey, Head of Production; Tom Yip, Project Manager; Amy Chen, Project Manager
LIGHTING Halo, Peachtree City, Ga.
PAINT Benjamin Moore, Montvale, N.J.
PHOTOGRAPHY A Frame Inc., Toronto

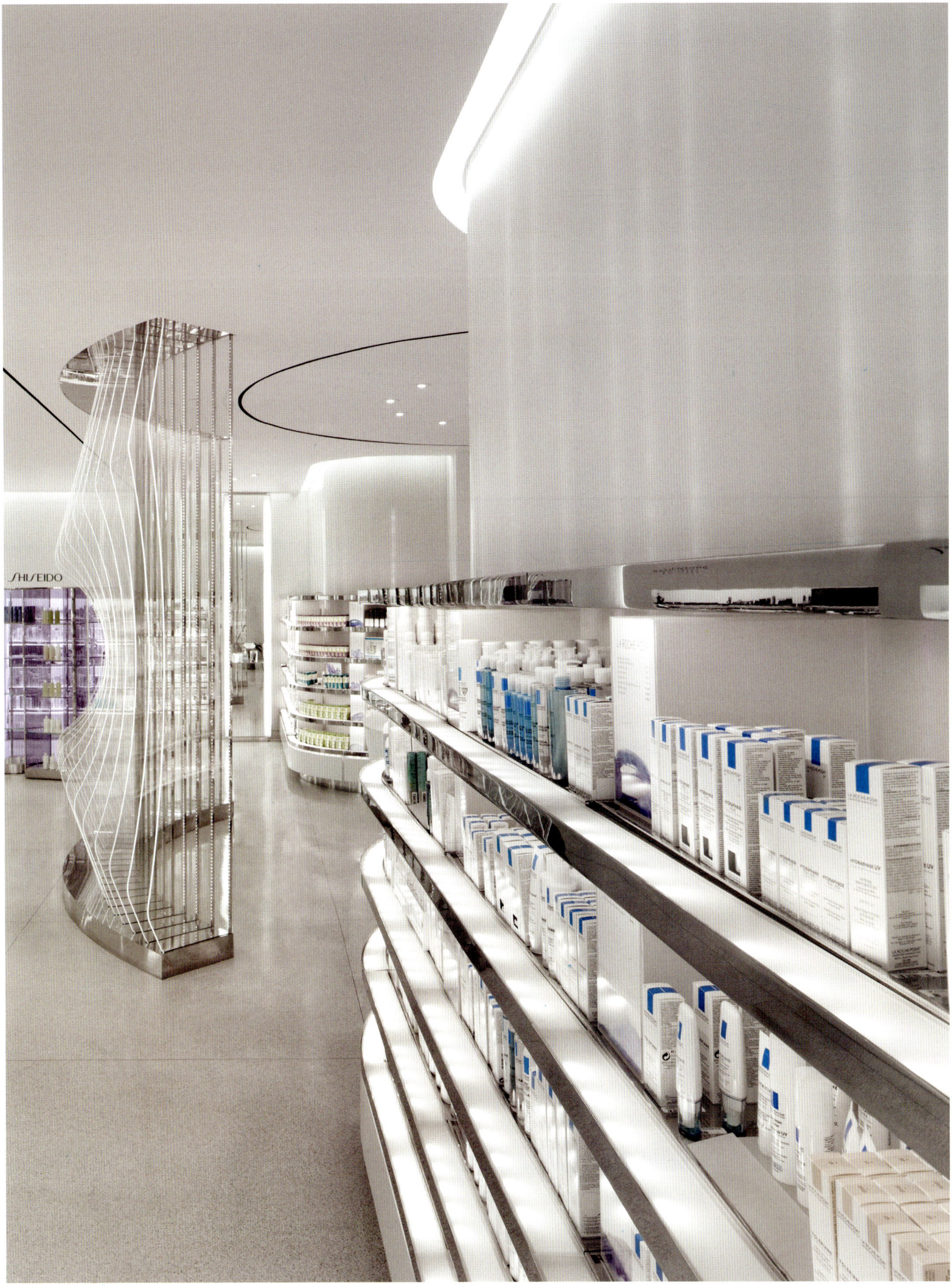
SHISEIDO

RALPH LAUREN
SEOUL

Award of Merit

The three-floor Polo Ralph Lauren flagship uses a more contemporary palette than its traditional look for this Korean location. The interior casework is composed of high-gloss white lacquer and stained American cherry. A focal staircase – which reads as a bold modern sculpture – is finished in white Venetian plaster and anchors the floating planes of each floor. Additional building materials include honed, rough-edged tumbled limestone flooring, drywall and Irocco wood-plank ceilings and fireplaces in Belgian black marble.

RETAILER Ralph Lauren, Seoul
DESIGN Michael Neumann Architecture LLC., New York; Michael Neumann, Principal; Jairo Camelo, Project Manager (Senior Associate); Kevin Eliseo; Richard Rogers; Benjamin Keiser
PHOTOGRAPHY JinKong Studio & Kesson Design, Seoul: Bong Chul Lee

STORES AND RETAIL SPACES 12

RALPH LAUREN

SEOUL

STORES AND RETAIL SPACES 12 **121**

DIESEL
NEW YORK

First Place

For Diesel's Fifth Avenue store, the retailer used rough metal and precious glass together on the three-story façade to showcase the character and history of the brand. The exterior's concrete and polished stainless steel contrasts with the warmer materials palette inside, which includes black steel and bronze. "Magic" mirrors in the dressing room use monitors to provide delayed images, so a customer can turn around to view her backside and see how the jeans fit. For the lighting, designers customized sleek, European-styled light fixtures to complement the texturally diverse interior.

RETAILER Diesel, New York
DESIGN Barteluce Architects & Associates, New York
PHOTOGRAPHY Daniele Minestrini, New York

STORES AND RETAIL SPACES 12 123

BARBIE
SHANGHAI

First Place / Innovative Concept

The Barbie Shanghai flagship that opened in China embraces Barbie's innate girliness, with 36,000 square feet of pink-and-white-tinged cuteness and bubbly energy. A three-story spiral staircase centers the space, encased in a display of 800 dolls from around the world. The store gives new meaning to the concept of "playing Barbies," with themed experiences that include the Barbie Fashion Stage, where girls get the chance to strut down the catwalk, and a full-service spa and café. Chute Gerdeman worked with Mattel to create the fashion stage as well as a Barbie Design Center, where girls create their own doll outfits from a huge wardrobe of options.

– Kristin Zeit

RETAILER Barbie Shanghai and Fashion Runway, Shanghai
DESIGN Slade Architecture, New York; Hayes Slade, Principal; James Slade, Principal; Emily Andersen, Project Architect; Tia Bauman; Tian Gao; Keith Greenwald; Jeremy Kim; Eliza Koshland; Chia-Ping Lin; Julia Malloy; Jeff Wandersman; Stephanie Wong; Rajiv Hernandez; Halley Wuertz; Palmer Thompson-Moss; Allison Weinstein

Chute Gerdeman Retail, Columbus, Ohio (Fashion Runway); George Nauman, Principal and Chief Marketing Officer; Cindy McCoy, Director, Program Management; Adam Limbach, Vice President, Brand Communications; Joanna Felder, Director, Creative Strategy; Bess Anderson, Director, Visual Strategy; Linda Krueger, Environments Designer; Steve Pottschmidt, Director, Design Development; Katie Clements, Trends and Materials Specialist; Mary Lynn Penner, Designer, Brand Communications; Matt Jeffries, Designer, Brand Communications; George Waite, Senior Designer, Graphic Production

PHOTOGRAPHY Iwan Baan, Amsterdam

SPECIALTY STORE OVER 10,001 SQ. FT. (TIE)

STORES AND RETAIL SPACES 12　125

BARBIE

SHANGHAI

126 SPECIALTY STORE OVER 10,001 SQ. FT. (TIE)

STORES AND RETAIL SPACES 12

WEST ELM
NEW YORK

Award of Merit

For the retailer's newest flagship on Manhattan's Upper West Side, designers created the illusion of a found space by designing an irregular perimeter wall pattern that shifts back and forth to create a series of interesting niche spaces. For instance, a loft becomes a focal point for a collection of end tables and chairs, where furniture is placed floor-to-ceiling on wooden shelves mounted on a wall of industrial backlit windows. Other alcoves within the 24,000-square-foot, two-story space feature individual products and elevated platforms for complete lifestyle displays. At the first-floor entryway, a series of shadowboxes flank the escalator and house furniture pieces and room sets, as well as seasonal graphics

– Sarah Fasce, Intern

RETAILER West Elm, New York
DESIGN Michael Neumann Architecture LLC, New York; Michael Neumann, Principal; Talin Rudy, Project Manager
PHOTOGRAPHY James Lattanzio, Montclair, N.J.

STORES AND RETAIL SPACES 12 **129**

WEST ELM
NEW YORK

SPECIALTY STORE OVER 10,001 SQ. FT.

STORES AND RETAIL SPACES 12 | 131

BLUSHBERRY
TORONTO

First Place

A hip, boutique setting introduces this frozen yogurt brand to Toronto's Queen Street West neighborhood. The store is clad in white mosaic tiles with a dotted pattern that echoes the brand's logo. A long bar within the 32-foot-long by 12-foot-wide space becomes a centerpiece where the product is prepared. The 18-foot bar and recessed lightbox are clad in Formica with a laser-cut logo pattern that allows pink LED lighting to shine through. White and mirrored walls add a sense of spaciousness, while storage spaces are cleverly concealed behind the bar with door panels that blend in with the walls.

RETAILER Blushberry, Toronto
DESIGN dialogue 38 inc., Toronto; Bennett Lo, Principal; Raul Delgado; Wendy Wang
PHOTOGRAPHY Jen Aurich, Toronto

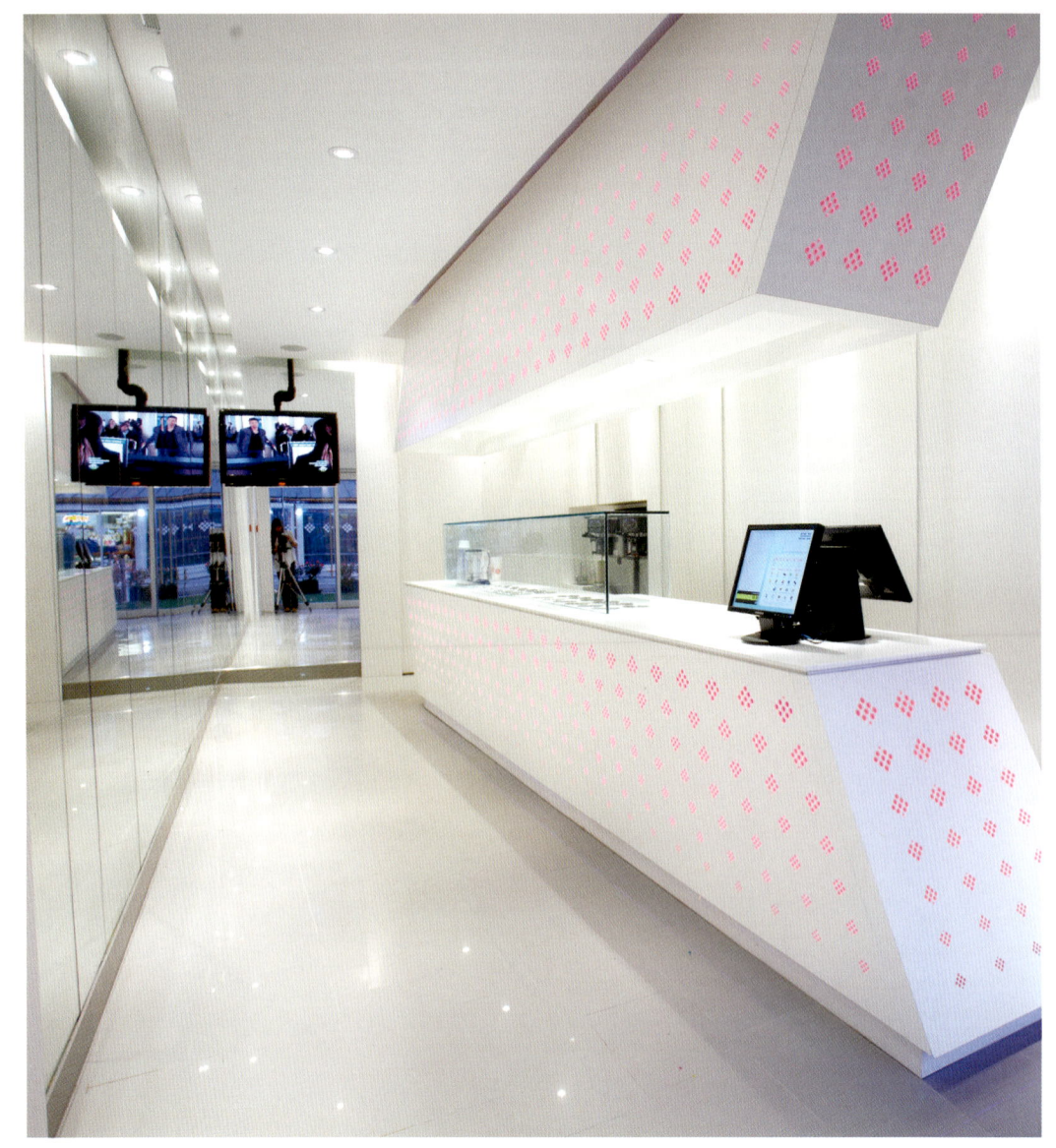

STORES AND RETAIL SPACES 12   133

PARIS BAGUETTE
SEOUL

First Place (tie)

With the goal to create a "little taste of Paris" in one of the world's most modern cities, designers used a mix of warm and natural tones and references to Louis XIV for the chain's newest location. The restaurant offers both takeaway and eat-in services, so products are placed on wall fixtures and island units to create a convenient shopping experience. Palatial chandeliers serve as ambient light sources, with spotlights adding a punch to product displays. Limed oak display tables, glass cake showcases and screens striped with transparent blue (in reference to the company's blue and white logo) add to the warm environment.

RETAILER Paris Baguette, Seoul
DESIGN JHP Design Ltd., London; David Rook; Darren Scott; Russell Castley; Raj Wilkinson
PHOTOGRAPHY JHP Design Ltd., London

STORES AND RETAIL SPACES 12 135

SPRING ROLLS - FAIRVIEW
TORONTO

First Place (tie)
Innovative Lighting Design

Following the remodeling of the Fairview Shopping Centre, the Pan-Asian restaurant chain refreshed its mall location using contrasting dark flooring and furniture with a white ceiling and sculptural walls. Running the length of the restaurant is an array of white MDF panels in rhythmic lines, with each panel protruding at different angles and varying joints. A 15-foot-by-4-foot lighting sculpture created from formed acrylic is illuminated with color-changing LEDs. Transparent red vinyl covered glass separates the bar and lounge area, which features illuminated red glass tables and bar stools.

RETAILER Spring Rolls - Fairview, Toronto
DESIGN dialogue 38 inc., Toronto; Bennett Lo, Principal and Designer; Raul Delgado; Marya Hwyn; Jericho Lee
PHOTOGRAPHY Eric Lau, Toronto

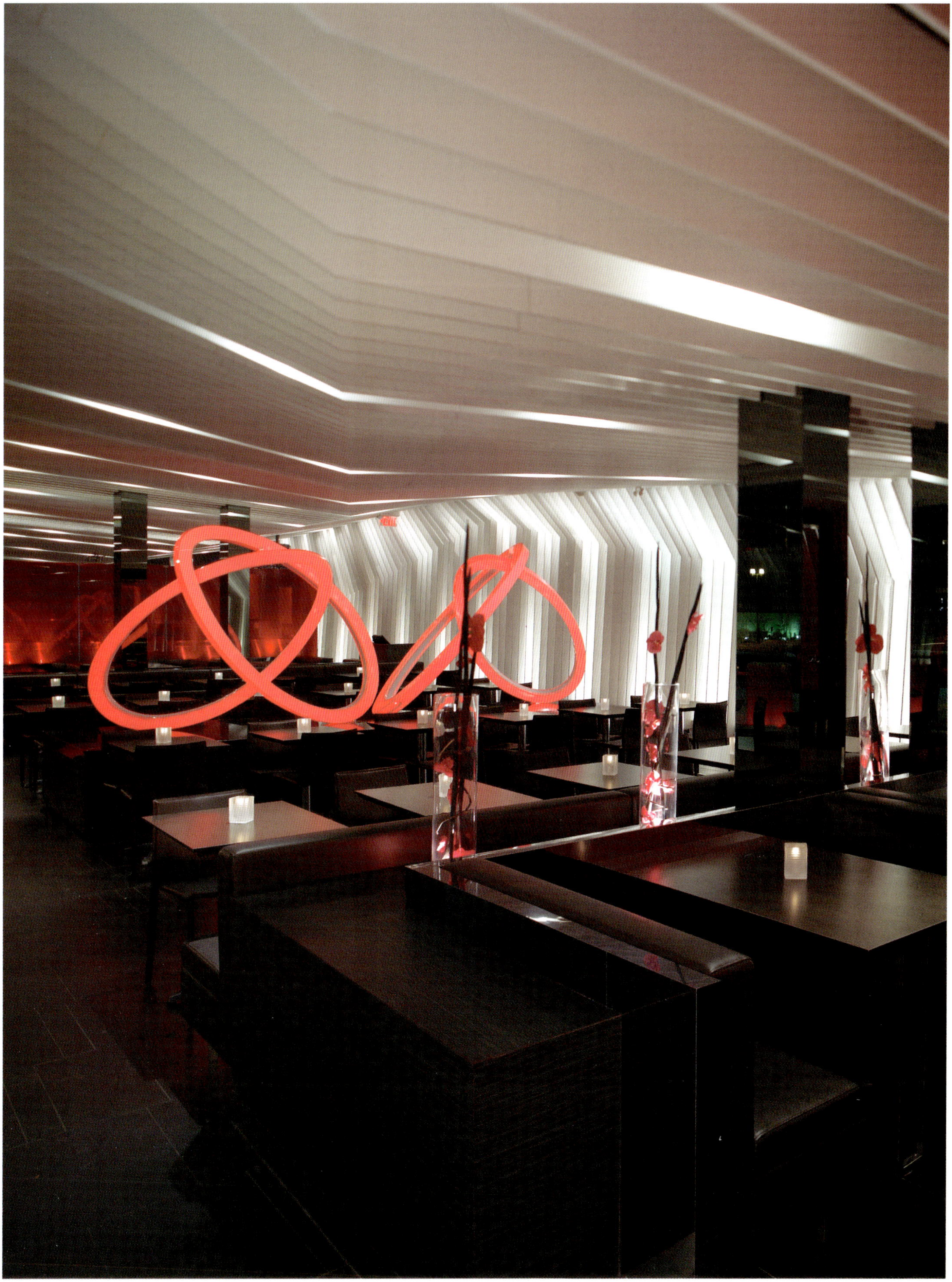

McEWAN
DON MILLS, ONT.

First Place

Celebrity chef and restaurateur Mark McEwan sought a high-end grocery store that captured the essence of his personality and love of cooking. Rather than putting fresh produce at the entry, the store experience starts with a curved wall highlighting the chef-prepared meal replacement offering. After that, customers journey through fish, meat, cheese and bakery departments before reaching the produce area. Finishes reflect an industrial kitchen setting, including polished concrete flooring and stainless-steel accents. Large-scale food photography emphasizing the quality ingredients, along with McEwan's family kitchen, are displayed throughout.

RETAILER McEwan, Don Mills, Ont.
DESIGN Perennial Inc., Etobicoke, Ont.
PHOTOGRAPHY Richard Johnson, Toronto

STORES AND RETAIL SPACES 12 **139**

McEWAN
DON MILLS, ONT.

STORES AND RETAIL SPACES 12 **141**

BRAVO SUPERMERCADO

SANTO DOMINGO, DOMINICAN REPUBLIC

Award of Merit

For its new ground-up hypermarket, Bravo sought a design and brand package that would differentiate itself from the local market using a European-inspired concept. On the exterior, full-height glazing exposes the multiple tiers of the store with visibility to the levels below grade. The use of ceramics, vibrant colors and graphics reflect the local Latin American art and culture. Signage is expressed graphically, with different zones identified by an artistic visual interpretation of the product rather than a sign with a name. Fixtures are in white, black and metal to keep the overall appearance clean and uncluttered. The project also showcases the brand's new logo, graphics, private-label packaging and promotional signs and labels.

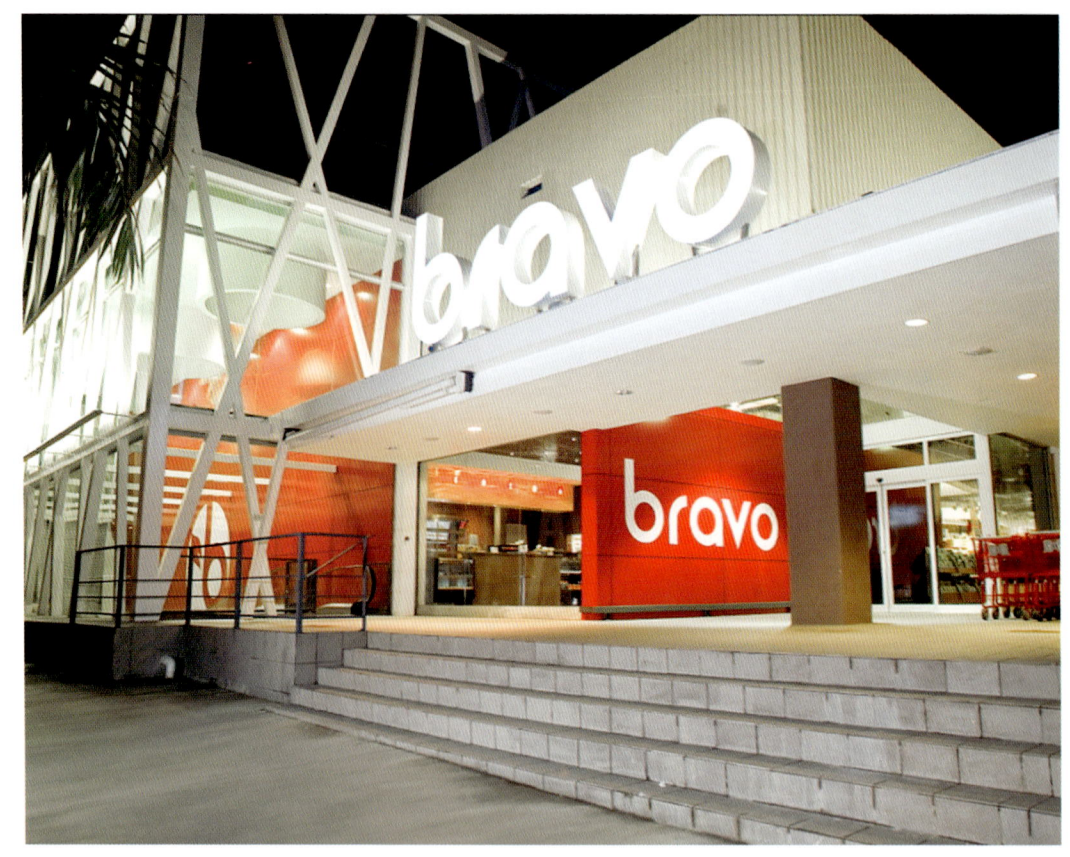

RETAILER Bravo Supermercado, Santo Domingo, Dominican Republic
DESIGN GHA design studios, Montreal; Nicolas Giammarco, Partner; Julie Dugas, Associate; Karen Currie, Senior Designer; Lynn Nees, Graphic Designer
PHOTOGRAPHY Estudio Fotográfico, Santo Domingo, Dominican Republic

STORES AND RETAIL SPACES 12 143

BRAVO SUPERMERCADO
SANTO DOMINGO, DOMINICAN REPUBLIC

STORES AND RETAIL SPACES 12 | 145

SOUK DU SOLEIL
TRAVELING IN NORTH AMERICA

Award of Merit

Global entertainer Cirque Du Soleil sought a merchandising strategy for its traveling "OVO" show. The "Souk" (Arabic for marketplace) had to address several challenges, including accommodating large crowds, providing flexible and portable fixture configurations and being able to be set up and disassembled quickly. The theatrical setting features draped Tivoli lights and ambient tent backlighting to give the space a magical glow. Finishes reflect a handcrafted artistry and include laminates paired with custom, powdercoated steel trims and fittings. Fixtures were developed based on a series of fantasy-like sketches and translated into pieces that are lightweight and nearly tool-free in assembly.

RETAILER Souk Du Soleil, various locales
DESIGN Miller Zell Inc., Atlanta; Keith Curtis, VP, Director of Design; Robert DeGroff, VP, Design Development; David Hawks, VP, Procurement; John Wilkins, VP, Senior Account Director; Scott Erwin, Creative Project Designer; Katie Janson, Creative Art Director; Sabrina Stinecipher, Senior Design Developer Director; Danny Corkran, Senior Design Developer Director; Jason Isbell, Senior Production Manager Director; Yancy Wilkinson, Creative Art Director
PHOTOGRAPHY Jiangnan Zhou, Montreal

STORES AND RETAIL SPACES 12   147

SASSOON
NEW YORK

First Place

The hair care company brought its updated European concept to the U.S. for the first time in an effort to create a consistent global brand identity. Challenged by a long, narrow space, designers turned the layout into a dramatic design feature using a saw-tooth layout of styling chairs and angled mirrors. Two light troughs run the length of the styling stations, while a glowing product wall was created at the entry. The dramatic color palette includes lots of white with a touch of dark wood, black and steel. A mottled, large-scale gray porcelain tile covers the floor. In keeping with the brand, the architectural signage is limited to a simple brushed stainless-steel vertical panel next to the entry door.

RETAILER Sassoon, New York
DESIGN TPG Architecture LLP, New York; Ron Alalouf; Juan Barraza; Alec Zaballero; Diana Revkin
PHOTOGRAPHY TPG Architecture LLP, New York: Alec Zaballero

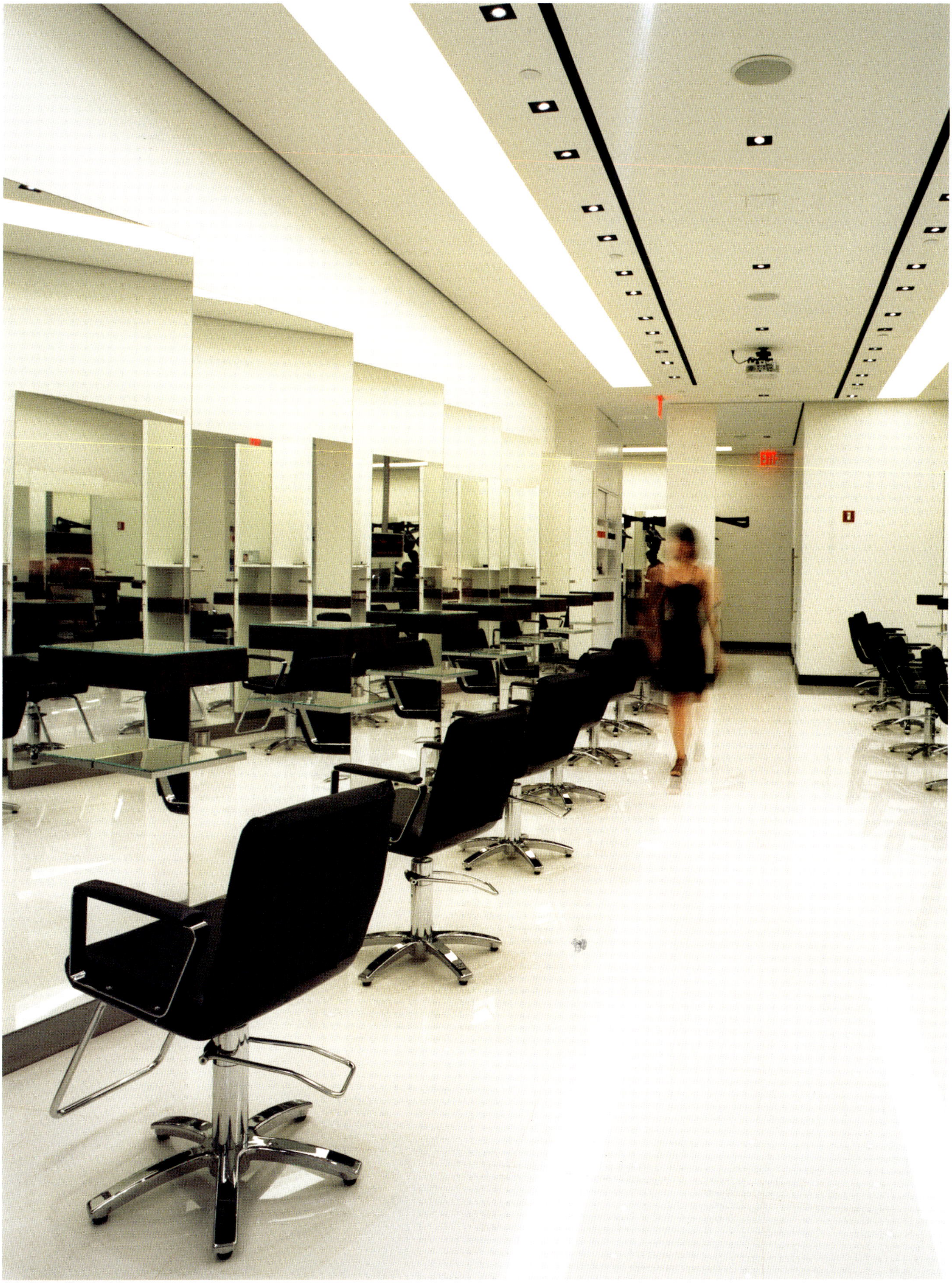
EXIT

FIRST FINANCIAL BANK

CINCINNATI

Award of Merit

This financial services setting was designed to create a new type of customer engagement. In keeping with that goal, the teller line is intentionally moved to a secondary position, communicating consultation over transaction. Clear views throughout the space dictate a "no place to hide" setting with transparent office settings. Interior graphics are transformed into walls that inform the customer, while aspirational imagery portrayed in graphics runs throughout the space.

RETAILER First Financial Bank, Cincinnati
DESIGN FRCH Design Worldwide, Cincinnati; Paul Lechleiter, Chief Creative Officer, Principal in Charge; Eric Kuhn, Creative Director, Specialty Brands; Toby Harris, Design Director; Alex Weber, Senior Graphic Designer; Katie Stepleton, Senior Interior Designer; Lori Kolthoff, Director of Resource Design
PHOTOGRAPHY OMS Photography, Cincinnati: Javier Jarrin

STORES AND RETAIL SPACES 12   151

SNAIDERO USA SHOWROOM

NEW YORK

First Place / Innovative Finishes, Colors and Materials

For this presentation of products for the kitchen, designers used a series of guiding elements, including staggered strips, lighting, floor tiles and structural columns, to lead to a focal point in the showroom where a collection of material finish samples are on display. Horizontal paneling with a special chalkboard finish wraps the walls of the corner office and the conference room. Here, visitors are invited to write messages as they pass, creating a space where the customer becomes part of the design.

RETAILER Snaidero USA Showroom, New York
DESIGN Giorgio Borruso Design, Marina Del Rey, Calif.; Giorgio Borruso, Principal Designer
PHOTOGRAPHY Magda Biernat, New York

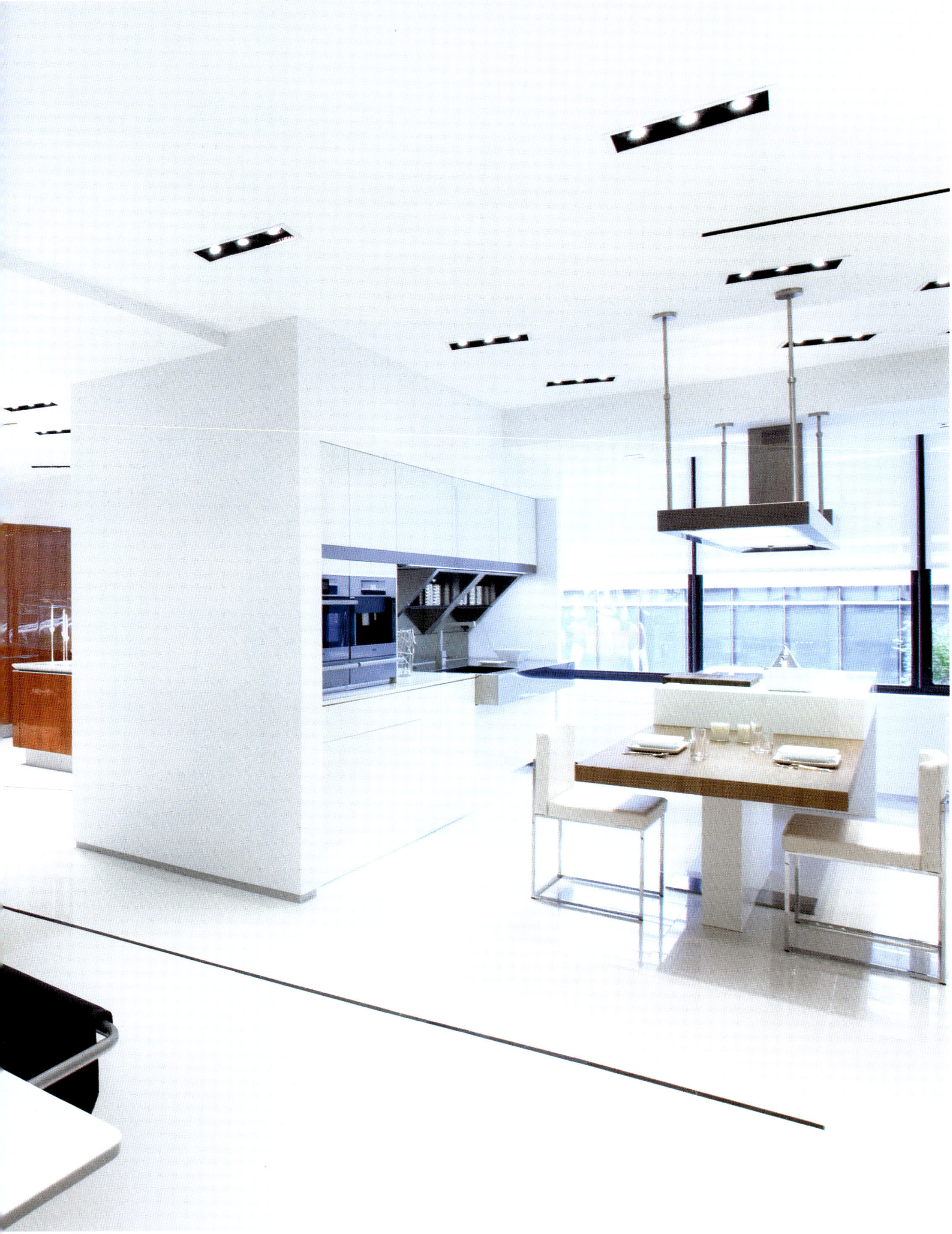

SNAIDERO USA SHOWROOM
NEW YORK

STORES AND RETAIL SPACES 12 **155**

FORNARI GROUP HEADQUARTERS
MILAN

Award of Merit

This 35,000-square-foot space houses showrooms, executive offices, storage and areas for exhibitions and events for the Fornari Group of brands. The geometrical construction uses a series of controlled curves carved into the walls, ceiling and floors, while seamless stainless-steel pipes diverge and converge along the outlines.

RETAILER Fornari Group Headquarters, Milan
DESIGN Giorgio Borruso Design, Marina Del Rey, Calif.; Giorgio Borruso, Principal Designer
PHOTOGRAPHY Alberto Ferrero, Milan

STORES AND RETAIL SPACES 12 **157**

WEST MARINE
JACKSONVILLE, FLA.

First Place

Rich with traditional nautical references, this store brings to life the adventure of boating. Its entertainment-based, lifestyle-driven design puts an emphasis on recreational water sports to appeal to a larger customer base, while the traditional fisherman is also comfortable shopping here. Departmental wayfinding is communicated through fabric sails and galvanized metal letters. Teak countertops, galvanized metal lamps, carpet tiles in a wave-like pattern and blue-stained and polished concrete floors round out the materials palette. Borrowing a cue from boating, the graphics are strung from cables and secured with products taken from the shelves.

RETAILER West Marine, Jacksonville, Fla.
DESIGN Chute Gerdeman Retail, Columbus, Ohio; George Nauman, Principal and Chief Marketing Officer; Cindy McCoy, Director, Program Management; Adam Limbach, Vice President, Brand Communications; Joanna Felder, Director, Creative Strategy; Bess Anderson, Director, Visual Strategy; Steve Pottschmidt, Director, Design Development; Katie Clements, Trends and Materials Specialist; Mary Lynn Penner, Designer, Brand Communications; Matt Jeffries, Designer, Brand Communications; George Waite, Senior Designer, Graphic Production
FLOORING Legacy Commercial Flooring, Columbus, Ohio; Constantine Commercial Carpet, Columbus, Ohio; Mats Inc., Columbus, Ohio; Daltile, Cincinnati
WALLCOVERINGS Rosul and Associates, Lakewood, Ohio; Crane Composites, Channahon, Ill.; Wolf-Gordon Inc., New York
WOOD WTP-Tabu Veneers, Hackensack, N.J.
PHOTOGRAPHY Mark Steele Photography, Columbus, Ohio

STORES AND RETAIL SPACES 12 | 159

WEST MARINE
JACKSONVILLE, FLA.

APPAREL

CHRISTIAN DIOR TEMPORARY STORE

NEW YORK

POP-UP/TEMPORARY STORE

Innovative Graphics

While its 57th Street was under renovation, the luxury retailer created a pop-up space slightly further Uptown, inside a former high-end boutique. Using the existing rhythm of the space, designers developed a series of room-like spaces for lifestyle product groupings, evoking a Parisian salon. Existing lighting was reused to accommodate schedule and budget. Surface-applied illustrative drawings create the feeling of custom interiors and architectural statements. Within the front entrance, a pedestal display with an interchangeable scrim establishes the brand's presence.

RETAILER Christian Dior Temporary Store, New York
DESIGN Gensler, New York
PHOTOGRAPHY Andrew Bordwin, New York

STORES AND RETAIL SPACES 12 **163**

CHRISTIAN DIOR TEMPORARY STORE

NEW YORK

STORES AND RETAIL SPACES 12   **165**

INDEX OF DESIGN FIRMS

212 Design Inc., 52-53

Aedifica Inc., 42-43

Barteluce Architects & Associates, 122-123

Burdifilek, 8-11, 92-93, 116-117

Callison/RYA, 24-27

Charles Sparks + Co., 100-103

Checkland Kindleysides, 44-45, 108-109

Chute Gerdeman, 48-51, 80-81, 158-161

Czarnowski, 84-85

dialogue 38 Inc., 56-57, 58-59, 132-133, 136-137

FRCH Design Worldwide, 20-21, 32-33, 94-95, 150-151

Gensler, 30-31, 162-165

Geyer Pty Ltd., 60-61

GHA Design Studios, 76-79, 142-145

Giorgio Borruso Design, 38-41, 82-83, 104-105, 152-155, 156-157

Hugh A. Boyd Architects, 64-65

ID& Design International, 14-15

II by IV Design Associates Inc., 72-75

Jeffrey Hutchison & Associates, 96-99

JGA, 34-37

JHP Design Ltd., 28-29, 134-135

LIT Workshop Inc., 12-13

Mancini-Duffy, 22-23

Michael Neumann Architecture LLC, 112-115, 118-121, 128-131

Miller Zell Inc., 146-147

Miroglio Architecture and Design, 62-63

Otto Design Interiors, 54-55

PDT International LLC, 16-19

Perennial Inc., 138-141

Ruscio Studio, 106-107, 110-111

S. Russell Groves Architects, 46-47

Slade Architecture, 124-127

TPG Architecture, 148-149

Watt International, 66-69

Wolfe Architectural Group, 70-71

Yabu Pushelberg, 88-91

For more information on visual merchandising and store design, subscribe to:
http://www.vmsd.com/subscribe (free subscription for qualified subscribers)

vmsd. Experience Retail Now

Books on visual merchandising and store design available from ST Media Group International:

Aesthetics of Merchandising Presentation
Budget Guide to Retail Store Planning & Design
Complete Guide to Effective Jewelry Store Display
Feng Shui for Retailers
Retail Renovation
Retail Store Planning & Design Manual
Stores and Retail Spaces
Visual Merchandising
Visual Merchandising and Store Design Workbook

To order books or request a complete catalog of related books and magazines, please contact:

ST MEDIA GROUP INTERNATIONAL

11262 Cornell Park Drive. | Cincinnati, Ohio 45242

p: 1.800.925.1110 or 513.421.2050
f: 513.421.5144 or 513.744.6999
e: books@stmediagroup.com
www.stmediagroup.com (ST Books)
www.vmsd.com (VMSD Magazine)
www.irdconline.com (International Retail Design Conference)